GREATNESS IS UPON YOU

SPIRIT REIGN
PUBLISHING
A Division of Spirit Reign Communications

HOW TO SEIZE AND SUSTAIN GREATNESS
ERIC THOMAS

Author: Eric Thomas
Cover design: David Anderson
Page design & layout Marie-Judith Jean-Louis
Illustration: Marie-Judith Jean-Louis
http://mariejudith.com

Editor: Eric Thomas & Associates, LLC
Publisher: Spirit Reign Publishing

© 2013 Eric Thomas & Associates, LLC. All rights reserved. No part of this publication may be reproduced, stored in a retrieval system, or transmitted, in any form or by any means, electronic, mechanical, photocopying, recording, or otherwise, without the prior written permission of the copyright holder.

Printed in the United States of America.

ISBN: 978-1-940002-37-8 (HB)
ISBN: 978-1-940002-38-5 (ePUB)
ISBN: 978-1-940002-39-2 (ePDF)

TABLE OF CONTENTS

Foreward..iv
Introduction...1
Week 1 Reputation vs. Character...8
Week 2 Getting Caught vs. Confession..28
Week 3 Victim vs. Victor..44
Week 4 Negative Thinking vs. Positive Thinking....................................64
Week 5 Grasshopper vs. Ant..84
Week 6 Minimize vs. Optimize..102
Week 7 Under Competition vs. Competitive Edge..................................118
Week 8 Currency vs. Legacy...132
Week 9 All About Me vs. Reciprocity..148
Week 10 Entitlement vs. Life of Science..164
Week 11 Lurker vs. Hunter - Round 1...182
Week 12 Lurker vs. Hunter - Round 2...198
Week 13 Lurker vs. Hunter - Round 3...216
Week 14 Sink vs. Swim..232
Week 15 Repel vs. Attract...246
Week 16 Stay vs. Go...258
Week 17 Extinguishing the Fire vs. Fueling the Fire...............................274
Week 18 Lost in Grief vs. Working Through Pain..................................292
Week 19 "Sometimes", "Maybe", "I'm Not Sure" vs. 120% "All In".308
Week 20 Beaten vs. Bested..324
Week 21 Desert vs. Vision...340
Week 22 Perform vs. Outperform..354
Week 23 Knocked Down vs. Bounce Back..368
Week 24 Wasted Information vs. Application......................................382
Notes and References..397
Acknowledgements..405
Thanks...408
Words of Greatness..410

FOREWARD

What you are holding in your hands is so much more than a book, it is an intellectual/psychological/ spiritual (IPS) map that has been created from real life experience ... a map that will guide you to a fulfilling life, from one successful adventure to another. Prepare yourself. Eric Thomas is right, Greatness Is Upon You! What you are about to read is filled with power, possibility and promise. However, you would be wise to remember that as true as that is and as much as you may believe it, no amount of reading or memorizing will make you successful in life. It is the understanding and application of wise thoughts that count.

Your spiritual DNA is perfect. It requires no modification, no improvement. The power that resides within you is far greater than anyone or anything around you. Eric has lived through this beautiful truth. He has experienced the highs and lows of life and has lived on both sides of the tracks. Like a professional astronomer, he has charted his experiences in such a meticulous manner that he is now able to share them with you. Eric's success can most certainly be duplicated by you through the application of the instruction he has so eloquently documented for your benefit.

I have personally been involved in the self-help industry for over fifty years and have watched speakers and coaches come and go. Those who have a solid spiritual foundation, who have lived and are living what they teach, stay, and become recognized for their contribution. Eric Thomas is here to stay. It is an honor for me to have been asked to write the foreword to his book.

In October 1961, I experienced a complete transformation in my life. I was given a copy of Napoleon Hill's classic *Think and Grow Rich*. With the book I was given a strong recommendation that I do exactly what the author suggests and not deviate from his instructions. Although I had previously never acted on good advice I'd received, for some strange reason I did what was suggested and my entire life changed like night and day.

This book can do for you what *Think and Grow Rich* did for me. I still read Hill's classic every day. Fifty years from now, if you can say the same thing about the book you're now holding in your hands, I can assure you, you will experience blessings beyond the scope of your imagination.

When I read Think and Grow Rich, my income went from $4000 a year to a $175,000 in one year and then I took it over $1M. Probably like you, I had been raised to believe you have to be really smart if you want to earn a lot of money; I found out that wasn't true. I was earning a lot of money and I knew I wasn't a rocket scientist. I was also raised to believe that if you wanted to get a good job, you had to have a solid, formal education. That also proved to be false. I only have two months of high school and yet, I not only had a good job, I owned the company and it was operating in seven cities and three countries.

I've earned millions of dollars and have had the pleasure of working with great men and women from around the world. I don't mention this to impress you, but to impress upon you that what you know and where you have been matters little in life. In my opinion, it's more important to know where you are, where you're going and from whom you're seeking advice. Seek advice from those who have done what you want to do … from forward-thinking people who push the boundaries and know anything is possible when you apply yourself. That is the message that you are going to burn into the deep recesses of your mind by studying the tremendous lessons in *Greatness Is Upon You*. Keep in mind I said by **studying** these lessons. Don't just read them once and pass over them like you're reading the newspaper. When a particular paragraph or page in this book moves you, read it over 100 times ... there's probably something in that paragraph that your soul is searching for.

I had the very good fortune of working beside Earl Nightingale and Lloyd Conant, the founders of the Nightingale Conant Corporation. It was a rich and rewarding experience for me and these two men became my mentors. Eric Thomas can be your mentor ... study him, listen carefully to what he says and do what he suggests. There will be great compensation in doing so.

Earl Nightingale taught me to surround my mind with greatness. He suggested that if I did this, some of it would rub off. I immediately recognized that was great advice. Over the years, I've gotten to know many great men and women, not by accident, but by design.

I am writing this foreword from my office library. I have about three thousand books on the shelves around me, books that I have studied over the years. I love great books. With a half century of experience in the success business, I have learned how to recognize a great book from just *another* book. *Greatness Is Upon You* is a book that will quickly gain a wonderful reputation and ultimately become a classic.

Read this book and do exactly what Eric suggests you do for 90 Days. By doing this, you will very likely continue doing this for the rest of your life, because ... Greatness Is Upon You.

Bob Proctor, featured Teacher in *The Secret* and bestselling author of *You Were Born Rich*.

THE BEGINNING...

I placed my head on the concrete floor of the cold abandoned building in frustration, thinking to myself, "This couldn't possibly be happening to me. This kind of stuff is only supposed to happen in movies; how can it be happening to me? I'm only 16 years old. How in the world did my life go from good to this?"

That was over 20 years ago. I can honestly say the winter of 1986 was probably the worst time in my life. I had managed to screw up my life while breaking my mother's heart and severing our relationship in the process. In addition to leaving home on not so pleasant terms, I further managed to get expelled from the Detroit Public Schools system and, worst of all, I was homeless.

If you would have asked me 20 years ago what happened and how I ended up in such a negative situation at such a young age, without hesitation, I would have responded, "It was my mother's fault! If she wasn't a teenage mom; if she had told me about my real father; if only my biological father had manned up and been present in my life; if only I had been born under more ideal circumstances... if only I had a better start... none of this would have happened to me."

But if you ask me today, I wouldn't take the easy route by, blaming my mother, father, or the circumstances in which I was born. As a man, liberated and changed, I would take full responsibility for my actions and the consequences I had to face during my most difficult years.

I see a lot clearer now, and I realize that it wasn't my circumstances that led me to make the decisions I made. There were thousands of individuals who were born under identical circumstances and some even worse who had not decided to handle it in the way I did. Looking back at my anger, feeling lost and confused at 16 years old, 20 years later, I realize it was my mindset, the way I viewed my circumstances that created the lane to self-destruction.

There was no denying the facts, my life had not been *no crystal stair...* I wasn't born with a silver spoon in my mouth - boundaries were created for me and limits were placed on me because of where I was from. But boundaries are meant to be expanded and limits are meant to be exceeded. Yet, instead of expanding the boundaries, I made excuses as to why I couldn't cross over them: instead of exceeding limits, I perpetuated many of the negative cycles that I would soon be trying to run away from.

Until one day, I met a man, a mentor, who challenged me to change my thinking so I could eventually change my life. A man who dared me to not accept the life that was given to me but to become courageous enough to create my own. Because of him, I began to see things differently, and I stopped making excuses and started making adjustments.

Maybe you're like me... or more, like I was. Maybe you've done some things that you're not happy about; things that you hope no one else knows. Maybe you've been abused or mistreated. Maybe you've lost someone you love to either death or a broken relationship. Maybe your rap sheet is full of missed opportunities, failed exams, or failed businesses. Maybe the sum of all of your adversities seems like a mountain...but mountains were meant to be climbed.

Now it's time to get over our past and the disappointments that came with it. Now it's about making the rest of our lives the best of our live's. Not only do we all have the potential to be Great, Greatness is upon you. As a student, Greatness is upon you. As a teacher, Greatness is upon you. As a spouse, Greatness is upon you. As a leader, an athlete, a nurse, a doctor, a politician, no matter who you are or your walk in life, Greatness is upon you - act like it.

The thing that I love about the Greats is their commitment to defeating the odds. Wilma Rudolph, Helen Keller, Walt Disney, Joan of Arc, Nelson Mandela, and Thomas Edison, to name a few, not only climbed mountains, they exceeded limits and expanded boundaries, setting the tone for those who respect and admire them.

My story of homelessness and being a high school dropout is not what attracts listeners to my message. And indeed, why would it? I'm not bragging about my past; had it not been for key figures in my life, things for me would be extremely different today. Still, what draws listeners is not the fact that I was on the streets, eating out of garbage cans, or that it took me 12 years to get a 4- year degree; what draws them in is that, like many of you, I wasn't living up to my full potential, and then I woke up one day and decided, "Greatness is upon me."

And it was. I can't believe that, 20 years later, I am a PhD candidate. I am married. I am the father of a high school graduate. I am blessed to be a source of inspiration for millions of people around the world. I received an opportunity to author a record-selling book, *The Secret to Success*. I am an educator. I am a mentor. I am someone who has managed to successfully defeat the odds. And so can you.

Greatness Is Upon You is where I rewrite my history. But more importantly, this is where you begin to rewrite yours. This is where you change your course from a life of disappointments, failures, broken promises, selfish ambitions, and mediocrity to one of self-fulfilling accomplishments.

Greatness Is Upon You is composed of 24 tried and tested principles from my own life. These are the keys to success that the Greats among us have used, and I have personally evolved as a result of each one of these principles. The next 24 chapters are going to help you get involved with changing your history and your trajectory if you commit to applying the principles to your own life.

These 24 lessons are formatted as an ascension program, a program designed to help you move from where you are personally or professionally to a higher level of performance. These lessons contain a mixture of narratives and excerpts from my life along with principles, techniques, and activities to help you grow and take your game to the next level, which, in turn, will help you to achieve and sustain Greatness in categories centered around personal and professional development.

Each chapter is sectioned according to the following format:

Day One: Learn It

The first day is structured for you to learn the principle and its foundations.

Day Two: Accept It

Plain and simple: once you learn the principle and the foundation behind it, you have to assess your life and accept how the information applies to choices you've made in your life.

Day Three: Embrace It

The activities on this day are just a hair of a step up from "Accept It", but this day is used to show you how your actions or inactions have or will truly impact your life.

Day Four: Change It

Once you've learned, accepted, and embraced the information, this day is spent either going one step further toward progressing to the next level or actually learning strategies that you can use to advance.

Day Five: Live It

Use this time to take personal ownership of your life - rid yourself of excuses and make adjustments. This day allows you to sit down and create your game plan for the week to put what you've learned in to action and apply it to your daily life. This is your plan based off of what you've learned in that week. It can include a more detailed approach at some of the activities you performed during the week, new strategies that you believe will work for your lifestyle, or you can repeat the whole week over again. (In fact, I suggest that you put each principle into practice for at least 90 days.) Whatever you do, use this day as your time to set the wheels in motion long term and commit to actually applying what you've learned to your life.

In addition, at the end of each week, you will find a "Greatness Is..." moment where I briefly mention a quote, story, company, or person in history that embodies Greatness. At the end of this section, reflect on what you've learned that week (you can do this directly in this book or use the GIUY Success Journal) and assess whether you met the challenge that was extended to you in that lesson.

You can start at the beginning or use the Table of Contents to determine the best place for you to start. And don't be afraid to spend extra time on a lesson - everyone's start and end point are going to be different. Still, over the next several weeks, you will experience moments of love, anger, laughter, and sadness. You will celebrate victories and overcome a few pains. But most of all, you are going to take all of these principles and learn how they work to help you live and exceed your potential.

Whatever your individual course, we all share at least one commonality - the desire to be Phenomenal at all that we aspire to do - and I am here to help you meet your goals one lesson at a time. Get your GIUY Success Journal ready!

We are about to embark on a journey of average to good to great to Phenomenal... Greatness is upon you. I hope you're ready!

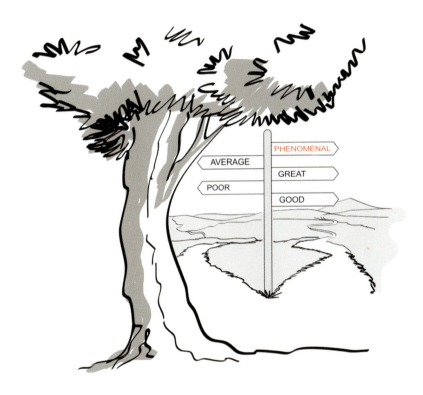

WEEK

01

WORDS OF GREATNESS

REPUTATION
a specific trait ascribed to a person or thing

CHARACTER
the combination of traits and qualities distinguishing the individual nature of a person or thing

REPUTATION VS. CHARACTER

Do you spend more time building and protecting your reputation or developing your character?

In the next two chapters, the distinction between reputation and character is highlighted. This week you will evaluate why people often value reputation over character and learn the importance of developing your core.

WEEK 01

"Character is like a tree and reputation like a shadow. The shadow is what we think of it; the tree is the real thing."

Abraham Lincoln

WILL THE REAL ___ PLEASE STAND UP?

> It seemed like an ordinary day.

It seemed like an ordinary day. I was sitting at my desk finishing up some paperwork for one of my clients to help him receive special funding for an upcoming project. Just as I was heading over to the fax machine, I heard a knock at the door.

"It's open," I said. It was my boss, Mrs. Paneros.

"Good morning, Eric," she said while standing in the doorway. "How are you today?"

Something about her smile let me know that, while she asked the question, she wasn't really looking for the answer. Still, I responded, "Things couldn't be better. Just getting ready to send this fax off, and then I'm headed out the door to meet with some of my clients before the program tonight."

"Oh ok, sounds great." she said. That's weird, I thought to myself. I knew she wasn't too fond of me spending so much time working on this particular program because she didn't see the value in it, and, normally, the very mention of it would send her into a series of socially acceptable convulsions. She never said it, but I knew she figured that if I was spending so much time working on a non-mandated program, that I couldn't possibly complete my mandated work at a high level.

"Can I see you in my office before you head out?" she asked.

"Sure, I'll be right up after I send this fax. Is everything ok? Do you need to talk about it now?" I pressed.

"Oh, no. Everything's fine, you can just finish up here, and I'll talk to you when you come upstairs," she said.

It seemed like an ordinary day. As soon as I finished sending the fax, I jumped on the elevator and headed to her office. When I got to the door, I noticed that it was partly opened. All I could see was her desk and the huge window overlooking an old creek that had dried up during the hot Alabama summer. Even though I was invited and the door was ajar, I didn't want to be rude and barge in, so I knocked. "Hey, Eric," she said as though she wasn't just in my office a few minutes ago, "come in and have a seat."

I walked into her office, completely oblivious to the reason she wanted me there to begin with. We had our differences before, but we hadn't had any confrontations in literally months. As far as I was concerned, the past was in the past and all was well. As I approached my seat, I noticed that she wasn't alone. On the other side of the door was her boss, Mr. Swanson.

"Eric, I believe you know Mr. Swanson," she said. I had met him a few times before at formal fund-raising dinners but never had any real dialogue with him. "Absolutely," I said, while reaching out my hand.

"He will be monitoring our conversation today," she said, positioning her glasses on her nose.

At that moment I felt the atmosphere shift.

"Mr. Thomas, we want to let you know that you are being written up for insubordination and purposely ignoring company policy. You're failing to live up to the expectations we had for you when you were hired".

I could hardly believe what I was hearing. Over the past year, I had worked my butt off to make sure the needs of my clients were met. I was arriving to work early and leaving late, taking on special projects and creating new ones, all the things that I was told were required as a part of my job.

"What?" I asked stunned, unable to wrap my mind around an articulate response.

"We've explained to you several times that there is a certain way in which we conduct business around here, and you continuously fail to meet the criteria." She then went on about how I purposely mismanaged paper-work in an attempt to make the office look incompetent. Then came accusations about how I had rallied some of the other co-workers in the office to rebel against her and her policies in an attempt to create an unstable work environment.

This was no longer an ordinary day. I couldn't believe what I was hearing! I could feel beads of sweat popping up on my neck as I grew increasingly angry.

"None of this is true, I ..."

"We have it all here in your files," she interrupted, "and we are going to be forced to go public with this and let you go. But if you confess to insubordination and submit your resignation now, on your own, you can walk away. No one outside of this room will ever know that we had this conversation. I would think this through carefully, Eric. The negative press and public humiliation that you could avoid alone makes my offer worth it. Take a few days to think it over."

This was the day that I learned the difference between character and reputation. Even though the next few days were full of rumors about the meeting and all the many implications, I didn't go out of my way to defend myself. Neither did I attempt to spit venom at my superiors for what I considered to be a misguided personal attack. Instead, I showed up to work every day with the same smile on my face, ready for the next challenge, unfazed about what could possibly happen or not happen if my reputation was slandered by lies and deception.

I would be lying if I didn't say that not worrying about my reputation was a harder road to take. When I was younger, I am confident that my anger and need to be seen a certain way would have gotten the best of me. But that day, I realized that there was nothing that I could say or do that would have more of a lasting impact than focusing on my character. I knew who I was, I knew my principles, and I understood that if I remained committed to those things, then nothing external to that made a difference; and so I decided that, for the rest of my life, I was done with feeding into other people's perceptions of me. From that day forward, whenever I was faced with a personal attack, I would let my character do all the talking for me. Let's just say that I walked out of the office, and my new strategy combined with my work ethic ended up working out. Within 11 months, I was promoted not once... but twice within the same company!

What's more important to you, reputation or character?

DAY ONE: LEARN IT

Look, I'm not trying to be deep, but in order for a shadow to exist, it needs something to give it life (i.e., a light source) (Fig 1). The same is true for reputations. Reputations need a light source - someone or something to give it life. This source can be gossip, low self-esteem, unresolved anger, deceptions, desires, disappointments, misconceptions, or misunderstandings. For example, someone with low self-esteem can have a reputation of being a jerk; a series of rumors can misguide people into believing someone is a thief when they really aren't. Because of this, you can have multiple reputations at any given time. When I was young, many people believed that I was skeptical, aloof, untrusting, and (because of my lack of interest in school at the time) unmotivated. For me, my father not being in my life cast a

> Reputations need a light source - someone or something to give it life.

shadow of insecurity and inadequacy that played out in my academic career and many of my relationships.

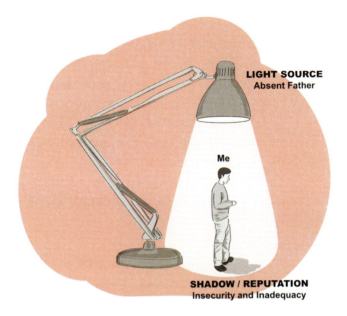

Fig. 1. Shadow Effect

Before I reconciled my relationship with my father, I had some major trust issues and submitting to authority was difficult for me. I was acting out because I was unhappy and this affected my reputation. But as my desires changed, specifically, after I met my wife, got my GED, and started college, I needed people to see me differently; I wanted people to think that I was strong academically; I wanted people to say that I was easy to get along with; and it became important that people thought of me as a "good" guy. My reputation changed, perhaps for the better, but nothing about Eric Thomas had changed. As harmless as this seems, I eventually realized that the reason I was so

> And changing the light source only cast a different shadow- it never addressed who I truly was at my core.

concerned with what "others" thought of me was because I wanted to be accepted.

My desire to be accepted would often times cast a shadow that was the exact opposite of the shadow that my absent father created. I went from having a "bad" reputation to having a "good" reputation. But at my core, I was still the same underdeveloped Eric, because I never addressed who I was inwardly; I only changed the light source. And changing the light source only cast a different shadow - it never addressed who I truly was at my core.

Fig 2. Changing the Light Source only changes the reputation

Let me make the connection: in the same way that shadows change in shape and appearance, depending on the type and location of light, reputations can also be shifted, people can see you as one thing one day and something completely different the next depending on the circumstances. But the interesting thing about shadows is that, even though you can see them, you can't do much more with them - you can't feel them; you can't hear them; and you can't smell them. As a matter of fact, if you take away the light source, the shadow no longer exists. This brings to question one thing: if reputations are like shadows, a mere facade of what truly exists, then why do we spend so much time trying to develop them?

> This brings to question one thing: if reputations are like shadows, a mere facade of what truly exists, then why do we spend so much time trying to develop them?

For me, not having a healthy relationship with my father created a void that I tried to fill by seeking attention and approval from others. So when I was faced with a situation that required choosing reputation over character, I chose reputation, because 1) I wasn't mature enough and 2) I didn't love myself enough to confront my personal issues that made me value what others thought of me more than what I thought of myself. I needed to work on developing my character.

> I needed to work on developing my character.

Becoming Great requires an understanding that character is paramount to your success, because, unlike reputation, character is consistent. It doesn't need a light source to survive; it doesn't hinge off of what other people say or believe; character is to your life what a steady foundation is to a house - build a strong foundation and the house will forever stand.

Are you able to distinguish between who you are and what people think about you? Before you move into this week's activities, prepare yourself by making sure you understand the difference between character and reputation.

DAY TWO: ACCEPT IT

Have you accepted the fact that your success is not about what people say about you but more about who you are?

CHARACTERISTICS OF REPUTATION AND CHARACTER

REPUTATION	CHARACTER
Temporary	*Eternal*
Rust	*Rust Proof*
Weak Foundation	*Solid Foundation*

Now, considering the descriptions in the chart above for both reputation and character, in your GIUY Success Journal, identify what people commonly say about you (your reputation) and then identify your principles/who you are at your core (your character). What are the consistencies or inconsistencies between the two?

DAY THREE: EMBRACE IT

It's easy to hide who you are on the outside, but each time we go through pressure the real you will come out. In my story about Mrs. Paneros, I had to embrace who I really was at my core, in spite of the temptation to try and save my reputation. Embracing my character worked to my advantage in the office that day, but the reality is that wasn't always the case for me. There are some situations where we need to embrace the fact that our characters need adjusting.

Character flaws don't have to be permanent. If you consistently behave or respond in a way that you know is unhealthy, unflattering, or otherwise detrimental, it is critical that you embrace the truth and do a self-assessment so that you can make the necessary adjustments.

> Character flaws don't have to be permanent.

Ask yourself:

- Am I consistently honest with myself and others about who I am?
- Am I loyal to my principles and values?
- Do I habitually invest in the interests of others?
- Do I take ownership for the mistakes that I make in life?

Few people can say that their answer to all of these questions is "yes" every single day. Some people deny that the "no" person exists - to their detriment. To get to the next level, you have to be willing to accept the good with the bad and commit to improving on the latter.

On Day Two, after listing those things that people often say about you, you should have listed your principles and core values - things that would describe your character. Today, describe those characteristics of yours that would be considered a flaw in character. More space is included in your Success Journal.

_____

_____

DAY FOUR: CHANGE IT

Trust is the catalyst for success. Many of us aren't able to get to the next level in our lives, because the people we are in relationship with (whether on the job, classroom, or at home) don't trust us. This is most commonly seen in situations where we represent ourselves as one thing when we are really something different. When people believe what you represent is truly who you are, you eliminate hesitation, doubt, fear, arguments, unnecessary contracts, and other time-consuming behaviors that will, in turn, increase productivity and your ability to achieve your goals. Learn to establish trust by strengthening your core:

> **Trust is the catalyst for success.**

- Make choices that coincide with who you want to be.
- Always apply the Golden Rule: Treat others the way you want to be treated.
- Embrace every opportunity to show people that you care.
- Take responsibility for your actions.

- No one trusts a cheat - play fair and stay fair.

Choose three of the areas you identified from Day Three, and create a game plan in your Success Journal detailing how you will work to improve in each of the areas that you noted as character flaws using the core-strengthening activities above.

I.E. AREA 1 : _____

_____

_____

DAY FIVE: LIVE IT

Are you ready to live a life that focuses on building your character more than your reputation? Write out your 7-day plan to live a life that focuses more on your character than your reputation.

Don't forget to use the core-strengthening activities listed in Day Four.

SUNDAY   *i.e., Write my 7-day plan ...* _____

_____

_____

_____

*Use your GIUY Success Journal to write out your plan.

GREATNESS IS...

Martin Luther King Jr. said it best when he said, "The ultimate measure of a man is not where he stands in moments of comfort and conveniences, but where he stands at times of challenge and controversy." Where do you stand in your darkest hours? Where do you stand when the very people you thought were in your corner are suddenly giving you up to the wolves? Where will you stand when you're faced with the decision between upholding your standard or buying in to the status quo?

You will never know the magnitude of your potential if external circumstances (your past, finances, people, your environment, etc.) have the ability to influence who you become. You will never realize success if your integrity is dispensable. You will never achieve Greatness if the measure of your worth is scaled by how often others praise or applaud you. Who are you when the stage clears and there is no one left in the audience?

What causes us to value reputation over character? Fear. If you never have to face who you are at your core, you never have to put in the work to develop it. We don't want to see the dark and the ugly, because then we have to make a decision to leave it there or change it.

Greatness is understanding that the bigger fear should not be in the realization of self but in its denial.

Spend time today reflecting on your actions this week.

Did you meet the challenge? If not, why?

_____

_____

_____

_____

SUMMARY OF THE WEEK

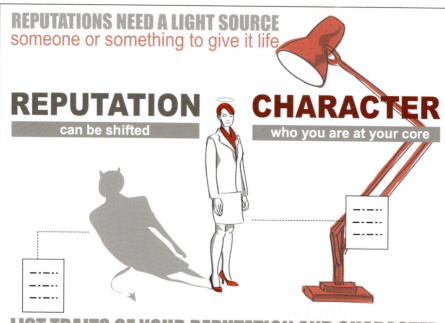

REPUTATIONS NEED A LIGHT SOURCE
someone or something to give it life

REPUTATION can be shifted

CHARACTER who you are at your core

LIST TRAITS OF YOUR REPUTATION AND CHARACTER

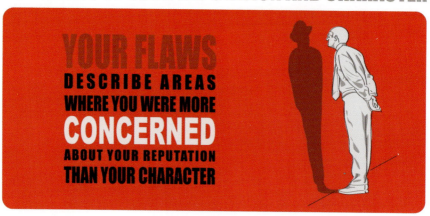

YOUR FLAWS
DESCRIBE AREAS WHERE YOU WERE MORE **CONCERNED** ABOUT YOUR REPUTATION THAN YOUR CHARACTER

HOW WILL YOU WORK TO IMPROVE IN EACH AREA?
create a game plan

GREATNESS IS UPON YOU
CERTIFICATE OF COMPLETION

This is to certify that

_____

has successfully completed this week's challenge.

Eric Thomas and Associates, LLC

_____
signature

_____
date

WEEK

02

WORDS OF GREATNESS

EXPOSE

To uncover or bare to the air

GETTING CAUGHT VS. CONFESSION

If you had to make a choice between confessing the truth from the beginning or waiting it out until you got caught, which would you choose?

In the previous chapter, I told you about the fickle nature of reputation and why it's so important to focus on developing your core. This week, we're going to take a closer look at what happens when we place a higher value on maintaining our reputation at the expense of our character.

WEEK 02

"Character cannot be developed in ease and quiet. Only through experience of trial and suffering can the soul be strengthened, ambition inspired, and success achieved."

Helen Keller

EXPOSE IT BEFORE IT EXPOSES YOU

When I was a kid, whenever I did something that could get me in trouble, I would immediately think of ways to avoid getting caught. For the sake of what I wanted others to think about me (my reputation), I would do whatever I believed I needed to do to project that image. If necessary, I would lie, hide, distract others, or anything else I could think of to keep the truth from coming out to protect my reputation. I did this for two reasons:

[1] I wanted my mother and her friends to perceive me as being a "good" kid.

My relationship with my mom was everything to me when I was young. Before I ran away from home, my mom and I were very close, and I loved to hear her brag about me to her friends. Being affirmed by my mom elevated my self-esteem, and having my name associated with good things made me feel good. So I would do things, uncharacteristic of my reputation, believing that if my mom never found out then she would continue to feed into the image that I was trying to project. I had fooled myself into thinking that I could build a good reputation without developing my character.

[2] I wanted to change the minds of anyone who didn't buy in to my "good" kid image.

Even when I would "accidentally" expose my negative actions, I would lie or go out of my way to establish or reestablish the image that I wanted to maintain. It was nothing for me to lie to my teachers and tell them that the signature on my report card was authentic or to help the principal get her bags into her car, even though she had just suspended me last week for cutting class. I desperately needed people to look at me positively, because I believed that a good reputation was going to benefit me.

But what I didn't realize was that while I was busy trying to avoid getting caught in an effort to preserve my "good kid" reputation, I was systematically causing further damage to my character; the more concerned I became with not getting caught, or not exposing myself, the more skilled I became at lying, hiding, and developing other destructive habits.

But the truth caught up with me. It always will. And when it comes out, the domino effect is explosive.

My character was exposed when I got caught stealing from the mall. I remember the day like it was yesterday. "Hands behind your back," the officer said, as he reached for his handcuffs and grabbed my shaking, sweaty hands at the same time. As he was walking me out the door to the squad car, of all the people in the world to see me cuffed with what seemed like an army of policemen, was my aunt. She literally called everyone we knew; and so the domino effect began. My mom was embarrassed and heartbroken; I was suspended for skipping school that day; everyone in the

> When you place such a high value on your reputation, you create opportunities for you to compromise your integrity and, in turn, damage your character.

community found out; my family was outraged and gave my mom a hard time; a barrier was created between me and my mom that strained our relationship and destroyed her trust in me; and I lost my "good boy" reputation. The truth was out. When you place such a high value on your reputation, you create opportunities for you to compromise your integrity and, in turn, damage your character. This is the ultimate consequence.

DAY ONE: LEARN IT

Last week, we discussed that reputations needed someone or something to give it life. My unresolved anger with my father for not being in my life was the driving force behind my reputation of being skeptical and untrusting, but years later, my desire to be accepted was the force behind my reputation of being a "good" guy. Reputations can be good or bad but are ultimately still unstable. For this reason, reputations and the circumstances surrounding them change so easily and frequently that any extensive effort in maintaining them can only result in catastrophic ends if your core is not strong. We've seen this phenomenon repeatedly throughout history.

To be revered as the fastest and the strongest, several professional athletes use illegal drugs to maintain their high profile images, only to have it crumble when the truth is exposed; this causes them to not only ruin the reputation they were trying to protect but also destroy their families and careers in the process.

Several times in the media, we've seen leaders of universities and churches exposed for criminal or fraudulent activities that many others were aware of but never disclosed the truth about, because they were more concerned about what the exposure would do for the reputation of the institution - they were willing to do some uncharacteristic things to preserve what others believed to be a reputable image.

> When maintaining your reputation fails you, what do you have left standing in the balance?

When maintaining your reputation fails you, what do you have left standing in the balance?

Remember, when I was young, I was so focused on making sure that people saw me as a "good kid" that I almost ruined everything with my lies and cover-up stories because they gave me a false sense of security. If I valued my character the way that I should have and worked on developing it, the lies, hiding, and stealing would have never happened to begin with. When maintaining my reputation failed me, I had nothing left in the balance - my "good kid" reputation was gone, it took years to rebuild my mom's trust, and my underdeveloped character was exposed. It would take years to rebuild the damage that was done to my character.

> I could have lied to protect my image from the lies that were being stacked against me, but by then I had learned that nothing corrupts your character more than a breach in integrity.

My ordeal with Mrs. Paneros in the previous chapter could have easily been a repeat of my childhood where I valued what others thought of me more than who I was at my core. I could have lied to protect my image from the lies that were being stacked against me, but by then I had learned that nothing corrupts your character more than a breach in integrity.

Remember:

- Reputations are like shadows - they are images that can easily be manipulated by external sources (i.e., people, gossip, unexpected circumstances, etc.).
- Character is who you really are - it can be developed or underdeveloped, but only you can control it.
- Reputations can be good or bad but are ultimately unstable. When more value is placed in maintaining or building your reputation than the building of your character, you risk compromising your integrity.

Think through these principles throughout the day.

DAY TWO: ACCEPT IT

Accept it. We all have (or have had) at least one group of friends or associates who we wanted to maintain a certain image in front of.

Maybe you want your boss and colleagues to believe that you're a high achiever when, in reality, you could really push yourself a little more.

Maybe it's important to you that your teachers and parents think you're doing well in school when, in reality, you've been cheating on your exams and copying your friend's homework assignments.

Identify at least one image that you have worked desperately to maintain and the things that you've done to keep that reputation.

DAY THREE: EMBRACE IT

Let's talk about the domino effect. I had to embrace the harsh consequences of working so hard to maintain my reputation when I was young. Below is an example of how valuing my reputation more than my character had explosive consequences.

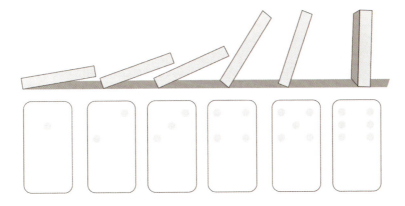

- Domino 1- I got caught stealing from the mall.
- Domino 2 - My mom was devastated.
- Domino 3 - Her friends found out and I became the talk of the community.
- Domino 4 - I was suspended from school.
- Domino 5- I embarrassed my family.
- Domino 6+ - My mom no longer trusted me. I lost my "good boy" reputation and had to fight to regain my mom's trust.

Identify a time when you valued your reputation more than your character. What domino effect did it create? Write out your domino effect in your Success Journal.

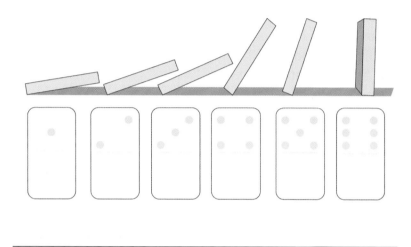

_____

_____

DAY FOUR: CHANGE IT

Unfortunately, many people don't realize the need to shift their focus to character development until it's way too late. Today, you are going to think of a way to intercept the domino effect and change what could otherwise be a catastrophic end.

This is accomplished by making a conscious effort to expose who you really are and work on developing that part of your core.

For example, instead of cheating on your exam, go to your professor or teacher and explain to him or her that you're having a difficult time in the course and need extra help.

Instead of immediately sitting up-right at your desk and switching the Facebook screen back to your data report the second your boss walks by, try actually working through the day without using work hours for personal time. Or instead of sharing credit for a project that you did little to no work on, publicly commend those who actually worked hard on the project, admit that you could've worked harder, and find out how you can legitimately contribute to the next project.

Notice that the switch to focusing on character development requires honesty with yourself as well as others. This is the difference between confessing and getting caught.

What will you do today to intercept the domino effect?

DAY FIVE: LIVE IT

This is your opportunity to invest in your core. How will you build on your character? Create a 7-day plan to move from valuing your reputation more than your character.

SUNDAY   *i.e., Write my 7-day plan ...*

*Use your GIUY Success Journal to write out your plan.

GREATNESS IS...

There's an old story about the son of a King who was instructed to go to war with their country's biggest enemy. This enemy had such hatred for the people of their land that the father knew that leaving anyone alive would ultimately lead to the destruction of their own people. So the father told his son to completely destroy the entire enemy army and all of their spoils - he was to take no prisoners.

The son desired more than anything to be seen as powerful and unyielding, and he had developed a reputation among his people as one to be feared. In war, the son battled courageously, but instead of instructing his men according to the directions of his father, he told them to leave the enemy's king alive. He knew that doing so would not only send a message to everyone in the kingdom about the extent of his prowess, but the enemy king himself would live to tell the story of how the son had defeated him and was gracious enough to leave him alive.

When word of the son's disobedience made it back to the King, he was sorely disappointed. As it was written, an infraction such as this was punishable by death. To sacrifice the lives and well being of his own people to be seen as powerful was deplorable. But instead of immediate death, the King ripped the son of all of his power and title. Devastated, the son went through a major psychosis, lost everything he ever loved, and eventually died in war. But worst of all, the long-term effect of the son's disobedience would soon be felt. The enemy king lived and, years later, the enemy King's offspring came back and destroyed all of the Monarch's people.

Working to maintain your reputation is possibly the most damaging thing you could do to your success. Character sustains what fictitious images won't. In the story, the King's son was willing to put his whole country at risk to have people think that he was powerful and, in the end, his shortsightedness cost him everything. What are you putting in the line of fire to protect what people think of you? Who are you willing to hurt? What are you willing to go through?

It's easy to say you don't care what people say or think about you, but do your actions reflect that?

Greatness is being courageous enough to not let what matters most be put at the mercy of what matters least.

Spend time today reflecting on your actions this week.

Did you meet the challenge? If not, why?

SUMMARY OF THE WEEK

WHEN MAINTAINING YOUR REPUTATION FAILS YOU
WHAT DO YOU HAVE LEFT STANDING IN THE BALANCE?

EXPOSE WHO YOU REALLY ARE
WORK ON DEVELOPING THAT PART OF YOUR CORE

IDENTIFY at least one image that you have worked desperately to maintain and the things that you've done to keep that reputation.

WHAT WILL YOU DO TODAY TO INTERCEPT THE DOMINO EFFECT

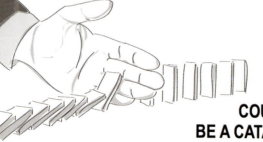

CHANGE WHAT COULD OTHERWISE BE A CATASTROPHIC END

GREATNESS IS UPON YOU
CERTIFICATE OF COMPLETION

This is to certify that

_____

has successfully completed this week's challenge.

Eric Thomas and Associates, LLC

_____
signature

_____
date

WEEK 03

WORDS OF GREATNESS

OWNERSHIP
the state or fact of being the owner or possessor of a thing

RESULT
the consequence of a particular action, operation, or course

VICTOR
a person who has overcome or defeated an adversary; conqueror

VICTIM
a person who is deceived or cheated, as by his or her own emotions or ignorance, by the dishonesty of others

VICTIM VS. VICTOR

Do you view the world in terms of what you've been slighted or in terms of what you can get out of it?

In this chapter, we investigate what it means to have a Victim's Mentality and how your thoughts significantly impact the results you get out of life. At the end of the next two chapters, you will know how to change your outcome with a simple thought.

WEEK 03

"A sign of wisdom and maturity is when you come to terms with the realization that your decisions cause your rewards and consequences. You are responsible for your life, and your ultimate success depends on the choices you make."

Denis Waitley

JUST ACCEPT RESPONSIBILITY

Honestly, I can't think of a disease throughout history that was more feared than the Bubonic "Black" Plague. I read that writer Giovanni Boccaccio, when referring to the disease, said "... [victims] ate lunch with their friends and dinner with their ancestors in paradise." This is how fast the disease moved. For several years, the epidemic tormented a whole Nation, and its aftermath reshaped the globe. Decades went by as neighbors abandoned neighbors, friends abandoned friends, and parents abandoned their children. People were running from the Bubonic Plague, because they understood that this disease was highly contagious.

This is exactly how we should respond to a Victim's Mentality.

If you see or feel anything within yourself that remotely looks like a Victim's Mentality, run from it like it's the Bubonic Plague! Don't allow yourself to become a victim of this illness. I am passionate about this, because I know about this disease what the people of the 14th Century knew about the Bubonic Plague - if you stay in the environment where the disease has manifested itself - then it's inevitable that you will die.

You will never experience real success if you live your life as a victim. Don't waste time and energy blaming others, rehashing past events, and soliciting unwarranted sympathy. Instead, make the necessary adjustments needed to conquer life's challenges. Success, meaningful success, begins when we take ownership and actively take responsibility for our part in the shortcomings of our life. This is the antidote to a Victim's Mentality... choose to live.

I admit that, early in my career, I hit a glass ceiling professionally. After my first five years on the speaking circuit, I became discouraged. I desperately wanted to get my message out to as many people as possible; I loved speaking to high school and college students, but I felt like my exposure was limited. I really wanted to speak to diverse groups such as corporations, graduating students, and international conferences, but the opportunities for those markets were few and far in-between.

For the longest time, I felt like I was being conspired against. I mean, what did the giants in the field have that I didn't? I believed that I had the passion, the delivery, the drive, and the personality to be a great motivational speaker. I thought that maybe my age was the issue, because I was only in my twenties. And if it wasn't my age, I thought that it had to be my background, because I was an African American male from a working class family and didn't have an affluent upbringing. In short, I didn't fit the privileged profile.

Eventually, I had to stop playing the blame game and start taking personal responsibility. Maybe it wasn't my age, but it was my immaturity... my inconsistency. Maybe if I spent less time playing video games, sleeping in, and watching every popular sitcom that came on TV and spent more time working on my craft by watching other speakers I admired, attending conferences, and researching techniques, the opportunities that I wanted would have made themselves readily available to me.

Maybe it wasn't my family's socioeconomic status; maybe it was the fact that, as a first generation college student, I failed to take full advantage of my college experience. If I would have applied myself in each course, I would have broadened my knowledge base and been in a position to speak at more diverse venues.

Maybe, just maybe, I was pointing the finger because it was easier to make excuses than it was to make adjustments.

DAY ONE: LEARN IT

In the first chapter, we discussed strategies that can be used to strengthen your character. Taking responsibility for your actions was one of the core-building activities, and it is possibly one of the most important steps that you can take in developing your character. Personal responsibility is having the courage under a myriad of circumstances to be accountable for oneself.

> Personal responsibility is having the courage under a myriad of circumstances to be accountable for oneself.

There is a difference between taking Ownership in your mistakes and disappointments, and playing the Blame Game. The reality is that there are times when external factors contribute to our disappointments but when we reflect and are honest with ourselves, we should see our role in the outcome as well. This is the one thing that people who suffer with a Victim's Mentality are not able to do; they can't see how their thoughts, decisions, actions, or inactions affected the outcome. As a result, they tend to blame others for their shortcomings.

> Our thoughts, decisions, and actions play a significant role in the results we get out of life.

Our thoughts, decisions, and actions play a significant role in the results we get out of life. While it was true that I wasn't getting the mainstream speaking invites that I wanted, it was also true that the things I allowed myself to think, decisions I made, and ways I behaved also fed into my disappointing results.

Fig. 1. Negative Thoughts Lead to Negative Results

For example, in the past I thought that I wasn't getting the calls I wanted because I was too young. I decided that seeking out corporate engagements wasn't worth my time and, in turn, I didn't seek out advanced opportunities. As a result, I missed several opportunities to speak in more challenging arenas.

> Victors not only admit to their mistakes, they make an attempt to make those mistakes right.

When I changed the way I thought about the circumstances surrounding my speaking career to something more positive, it enabled me to make better decisions and eventually led to more favorable results.

Fig. 2. Positive Thoughts Lead to Positive Results

When I changed, I began to think, "If I work on my craft more, I'll get better results." I decided to hone my energy into studying more experienced speakers and, in turn, stepped up my game at the speaking engagements I was booked for. As a result, more people began to admire my work, and the bigger events I was looking for finally came.

I moved from being a Victim to a Victor.

Being a Victor isn't always about winning. It's about conquering the temptation to believe that you aren't where you want to be because of what others did to you. Victors not only admit to their mistakes, they make an attempt to make those mistakes right. They don't make excuses, they make adjustments.

Consider the challenges and disappointments you presently face in your life.

What role did/do you play in them? What was your thought process throughout this difficult time? What decisions did you ultimately make? How did these decisions affect the outcome? What could you have done differently to achieve a more positive result?

Let's say, for argument's sake, that your challenges can be divided into two categories: challenges you can manipulate and challenges that are out of your control.

I told you, it took me 12 years to get a 4-year degree; some things were out of my control, but I had to accept those challenges that I had that I could've easily changed.

Make a list of the most devastating challenges that have had an impact on your personal or professional life (i.e., fired from a job/death of a loved one), and place each major challenge under one of the areas below.

CHALLENGES THAT ARE OUT OF YOUR CONTROL	CHALLENGES THAT YOU CAN MANIPULATE
i.e., I was a first generation college student.	1. I didn't utilize my resources. 2. I didn't put forth my best effort in college. 3. I didn't ask for help when I needed it.

How did the challenges you can manipulate help you to develop or hinder you personally or professionally?

_____

_____

Now that you've gone through these exercises, hopefully you can understand how concentrating on what you can control versus what you can't control can empower you. In what ways in your professional life can this view point assist you now?

_____

_____

DAY TWO: ACCEPT IT

Yesterday, you learned the difference between being a Victim and Victor and reflected on the disappointments you presently face in your life. Today, challenge yourself to accept your role in one or more of the disappointments, so that you can begin the process of creating ownership for your actions.

Remember, in my example earlier, a major disappointment for me was that I wasn't getting the speaking invites that I wanted. At that time, I was thinking that it was because of my age, economic status, and limited opportunities. As a result, I decided to not pursue certain venues in fear of rejection, and I potentially missed out on several opportunities.

One major disappointment in my life was when...
___

___

During this time, I was thinking ...
___

___

My actions involved me...
___

___

As a result, I...
___

___

One Step Further: If you are a visual learner, you can do the same activity above by placing your answers in a diagram similar to the one below:

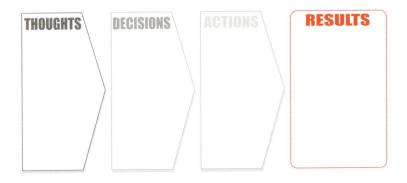

Example of a Disappointment: "I didn't get the promotion I wanted."

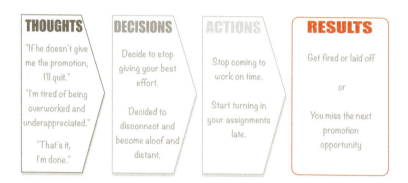

DAY THREE: EMBRACE IT

Most times when things don't go well, we think in the frame of:

I would have been able to do

_____

if

_____

had done his/her part

or

This would not have happened if it weren't for

_____

Today, you are going to practice taking ownership for the role you played in your tragedy.

Look at yourself in the mirror (i.e., bathroom mirror, handheld mirror, hallway mirror, etc.) and verbally admit to yourself your role in the disappointment you wrote about yesterday. Explain to yourself how your behavior led to the end results.

Example: "I was fired from my job, because I got upset about not getting the promotion I wanted; I stopped giving my best effort at work and started coming in late."

Repeat your sentence to yourself in the mirror 3 times while looking at yourself square in the eyes.

Acknowledge and receive what you are saying to yourself and commit to not making the same mistake again. Don't forget to think about what thoughts, decisions, and actions would have led to more positive results.

Remember, the Victim vs. Victor perspective vastly affects our success.

DAY FOUR: CHANGE IT

Now that you have courageously looked at yourself in the mirror, it's time to commit to a change.

There are definitely times when other people play a role in our disappointments. It's ok to acknowledge this as long as we have taken the time to look at how our own actions led to the upset. After you've looked at yourself in the mirror (as you did yesterday), it is safe to now consider the other players involved.

It has been said that when Abraham Lincoln had an issue with someone, he would take out his quill and write them a letter. Depending on the circumstances, he would write the same letter 2, 3, and sometimes 4 times, setting a match to each one as he completed it. This method proved effective in getting unresolved feelings out of his system and I believe it was instrumental in his growth.

Today, write a letter to the other player(s) involved in the disappointment that you have been focusing on this week (i.e., your boss, your teacher/professor, an old friend, spouse, etc.). Identify both of your roles in the disappointment and be honest about how the situation made you feel. Don't be afraid to write this letter 3, 4, or even 5 times if necessary. I DO NOT recommend that you burn the letters, but ball each one up and throw them away as you finish. Remember, the goal is not to deliver this letter but to get unresolved feelings out of your system. Sometimes change simply involves handling things in a way you never would have considered before. This assignment is meant to be a therapeutic means for you to get some things out of your system that may be holding you back from becoming a Victor.

DAY FIVE: TEACH IT

Write a 7-day plan to shift from victim to victor.

Consider things in your life that you do habitually that have contributed to upsets on a consistent basis. Before you begin your journey, go back to the same mirror you stood in front of earlier this week, and vow to make the necessary changes to your character.

SUNDAY   *i.e., Write my 7-day plan ...*

_____

*Use your GIUY Success Journal to write out your plan.

GREATNESS IS...

Albert Einstein said that "man must cease attributing his problems to his environment, and learn again to exercise his will – his personal responsibility."

What if Einstein, in the midst of being underestimated by his teachers, being misunderstood at home and in school, and having a father who had multiple failed businesses, saw himself as a mere victim in a world of a series of unfortunate life-altering events? What if he waited for his professors to affirm his intellect? What if he made a commitment to resentment instead of responsibility? What if he stifled his gifts and talents so that he could instead voice his discontentment with the people in his environment? What if Einstein chose to blame his parents' failures for his own failures and became content with mediocrity at the expense of Greatness?

The answer is simple: we would be acknowledging someone else for revolutionizing the way we see science.

We are all one complaint or rationalization away from someone else doing what you were meant to do. Because while you're wasting time complaining and placing blame on other people and circumstances, someone else is exercising his or her will and taking responsibility for his or her actions so that he or she can claim Victory out of life and not be victimized by a defeatist mentality.

Greatness is being courageous enough to acknowledge your role in all that is wrong in your life and disciplined enough to not let it keep you from moving forward.

Spend time today reflecting on your actions this week.

Did you meet the challenge? If not, why?

_____

_____

SUMMARY OF THE WEEK

VICTIM PLAYING THE BLAME GAME

VS

VICTOR TAKING OWNERSHIP

Our thoughts, decisions, and actions play a significant role in the results we get out of life.

CHALLENGES AND DISAPPOINTMENTS

What role did/do you play in them?

What was your thought process throughout this difficult time?

What decisions did you ultimately make?

LOOK AT YOURSELF IN THE MIRROR
ADMIT YOUR ROLE IN YOUR DISAPPOINTMENT

GET UNSOLVED FEELINGS OUT OF YOUR SYSTEM

WRITE A LETTER TO THE OTHER PLAYER(S) INVOLVED IN THE DISAPPOINTMENT THAT YOU HAVE BEEN FOCUSING ON

GREATNESS IS UPON YOU
CERTIFICATE OF COMPLETION

This is to certify that

_____

has successfully completed this week's challenge.

Eric Thomas and Associates, LLC

_____
signature

_____
date

WEEK 04

WORDS OF GREATNESS

THOUGHT
the ideas or arrangement of ideas that result from thinking

NEGATIVE THINKING VS. POSITIVE THINKING

From where you stand, is the glass half full or not even worth the effort?

In the previous chapter, we discussed that the way you think has a significant impact on the results that you get out of life. In this chapter, we take a closer look at the effects of negative thinking and how you can systematically deprogram from habitual negative thinking to positive thinking.

WEEK 04

"The worst disability in life is a bad attitude."

Supa Nova Slom

LET THIS MIND BE IN YOU

"I'm telling you, these parents don't give a damn about these kids. If they did, I wouldn't have to call them a million times just to get them to come up to this school and see why their son or daughter is failing Algebra! But the minute I take away their child's cell phone or game system, they're at the school before the doors open - it's ridiculous!"

These were the frustrated sentiments of a friend of mine who was a teacher at an inner city school in Atlanta as she was packing her briefcase to head to a faculty meeting.

"I mean, I get so tired of having to listen to administrators every other day telling me how I should run my classroom and questioning why my test scores are so low, and yet I don't see any of them coming up with solutions as to how I can get these parents to come up to this school and take an interest in their children. Meanwhile, I spend close to half of each period addressing behavior issues that I shouldn't have to address, and the other half reteaching material that they should have learned from their teachers last year. I'm so tired of this. I don't even know why I try. I am not doing this again next year."

I've been doing teacher trainings and educational workshops for well over a decade in multiple regions across the country, and what I knew about my friend and her experiences was that some of the anger and frustration she felt was valid. But the biggest issue here wasn't the lack of parental involvement or an unsupportive administrative staff. The issue was her attitude - her mindset about her experiences as a teacher.

You have heard me say it a million times: Success is a mentality – it's a way of life. Because your mindset is long lasting, every single thing that you do has to be done as an extension of your mindset if you plan to succeed. For my friend, this meant that her ability to be successful at teaching in her environment (and her quality of life) would depend on her mindset - the way she allowed herself to think. One of my favorite creeds states, "As a man thinketh so is he..." This means that your actions are a direct reflection of the way you think. My friend was getting ready to walk out on her job, a decision that may have been well justified, but if you look a little deeper, her attitude was definitely a key player in getting her out of the door. She was looking at her job from the perspective of what the school could do to make it better, or what could others do to make it better and not in terms of what she could do to make it better. It was her mindset. If you think like a person who is fed up and disgusted, you're going to see your experiences based off of how you think.

It may sound weird, but my metamorphosis started the day I began to think about my thinking. I learned from the late great motivator himself, Zig Ziglar, that a person's thoughts could be categorized in two ways: "stinking thinking" or "positive thinking." Prior to that, I would have to say I never really gave much thought about my thoughts, or how they dictated my behavior and affected the quality of my life.

Success is very deliberate and therefore our thoughts must be also

But the fact is, our lives can change for the better by making small mental adjustments. These mental adjustments determine whether you live your life as a Victim or a Victor. My friend believed that she was stuck because her students' parents were uninvolved and the school administrators weren't supportive. Not only did I not hear her take any ownership in what was happening with her students, everything that came out of her mouth was negative. She was playing the blame game, pointing fingers at everybody else, and we learned last week how dangerous that is.

Negative thinking is a major component of a Victim's Mentality and ultimately makes it difficult for you to strengthen your character. This is counterproductive to Greatness.

DAY ONE: LEARN IT

Success is very deliberate, and therefore our thoughts must be also. Like a raindrop to a river, our thoughts drive our actions and shape our life outcomes. We must learn to:

- Be aware of what we think (be conscious of our thoughts).
- Understand how our thoughts shape our reality (and eventually our destiny).

- Be more intentional about the direction we allow our minds to go. Meaning, when you catch yourself thinking negatively, STOP. REDIRECT to something positive.

> The move toward being phenomenal in any aspect of your life begins and ends with one simple thought.

When we were making the distinction between Victor and Victim, we discussed that a Victim's Mentality begins with the way we allow ourselves to think. Negative thinking not only creates stress, it compounds it, thus making it difficult to make decisions and act in a way that would promote our ability to succeed. The move toward being Great in any aspect of your life begins and ends with one simple thought.

What mental adjustments do you need to make to better position yourself in your career, academic life, social life, or family life? For example, prior to the birth of my son, Jalin, school and I had an antagonistic relationship - I hated it and thought it hated me. As a result, I left undergrad with a 1.7 GPA. Jalin's birth forced me to think about school in a way I had never considered before; once I did, I went back to school and began to see dramatic changes in my GPA. Changing my mind about school positioned me for success.

> Changing my mind about school positioned me for success.

Are you able to see how your thoughts affect your behavior?

DAY TWO: ACCEPT IT

Accepting that your thoughts influence your actions may be difficult, but I challenge you to look deeply at some areas in your life that aren't going well to see if you can find some commonalities in the type of thinking that you're doing and the outcome. Follow the steps below to complete the diagram for an area in your life that you are currently experiencing a CHALLENGE in when it comes to the way you think:

- IDENTIFY your CHALLENGE area.
- Describe the thoughts that you commonly have in that area.
- Describe the things that you commonly say concerning that area in your life. (This can be things that you say to other people or things that you say to yourself.)
- Describe your behavior in that area (use action words).

Challenge Area

_____

CURRENT

THINK ABOUT IT

SPEAK ABOUT IT

BE ABOUT IT

DAY THREE: EMBRACE IT

The way we speak, think, and behave gives others an impression of our attitude. Even if you are completely justified, the wrong impression can be extensively damaging to your success. What if my friend's principal had walked in on her during her rant? Or worse yet, what if a student had heard her? She wouldn't have needed to worry about quitting, she would have been fired with a damaged image to boot. The truth is, we can't control the thoughts and actions of others, but we will always be held accountable for our own words, thoughts, and actions because we are in the best position to control them.

> Even if you are completely justified, the wrong impression can be extensively damaging to your success.

Yesterday you identified an area in your life that was adversely affected by your negative thinking. Today, you're going to look at that same situation and think through positive ways to think, speak, and ultimately behave in that situation.

For example:

Thinking - How can you think differently to reposition yourself for success in your CHALLENGE area from yesterday?

If you normally spend your work day thinking, "I can't wait until its time to go home," instead try thinking, "I wonder how much work I can get done from now until its time to go home."

Speaking - How can you speak differently to reposition yourself for success in your CHALLENGE area from yesterday?

If you are a teacher and you normally talk to other teachers about your negative encounters with a certain student in your classroom, try instead to speak about the positive things that the student has done in your classroom. Or if you normally engage in gossip about your boss, professors, or colleagues, try instead to change the topic or, again, say something positive about the person instead.

People underestimate the power of positivity. But the truth is that when you are known as the one who is always speaking positive, people are less likely to come to you with their negative energy and, in turn, you are less likely to be involved in conversations that will tempt you to speak negatively.

Behaving - What can you physically do differently to reposition yourself for success in your CHALLENGE area from yesterday?

Offer to take your employee out for lunch instead of making him or her work through the lunch hour. Or do something nice for a member of your team or organization who usually annoys you.

- IDENTIFY your CHALLENGE area from Day Two.
- Describe the positive thoughts that you should have in that area.
- Describe the things that you should say concerning that area in your life.

- Describe what your behavior should look like in that area.

Be sure to think through how your thoughts and language should change in order to see a successful change in your behavior.

CHALLENGE AREA

_____

POSITIVE CHANGE

THINK ABOUT IT

SPEAK ABOUT IT

BE ABOUT IT

DAY FOUR: CHANGE IT

Now that you've thought of ways to change your thinking, speaking, and behavior (Day Two), address what general changes in your speech and actions/behaviors you and the people around you can expect to see as a result of your decision to engage in more positive thoughts.

In your GIUY Success Journal, list the different changes in your speech that you plan to make and the actions you can commit to changing on the regular.

SPEAKING	WHAT ACTIONS WILL I SEE AS A RESULT OF THE CHANGES ?
i.e., I will speak more positively about my student's behavior.	*I won't be as frustrated with my student and my positive attitude will have a lasting impact on my student as well as my colleagues.*

DAY FIVE: LIVE IT

Create a 7-day plan for how you will actively work to change the way that you think. Be sure to include extra meditation and reflection time in your plan so that you can learn what negative thoughts trigger your negative behaviors.

SUNDAY   *i.e., Write my 7-day plan ...*
_____

*Use your GIUY Success Journal to write out your plan.

Greatness Is...

"Either make the tree sound (healthy and good), and its fruit sound (healthy and good), or make the tree rotten (diseased and bad), and its fruit rotten (diseased and bad); for the tree is known and recognized and judged by its fruit ." [Matthew 12:33 Amplified Bible]

The reason we fall prey to negative thinking is because it's easy.

When the children are getting on your nerves; when your boss doesn't notice your hard work; when you didn't get accepted into the school or program you dreamed of getting into; when your employees don't seem to get the vision of the company and productivity is slow; when the bills are piling up; when you're still looking in the face of unemployment; when the doctors have given you bad news; when you're fed up, tired, and lonely the most comfortable place in the world is Pessimism. It quenches the thirst of disappointment.

Positive thoughts in the midst of struggles are challenging because it forces you to consider and then believe that which is invisible in the moment of your trial. Either make the tree sound and let it Bear good fruit or make it rotten and let it Bear bad fruit. Life isn't easy so the way that you process it isn't going to be either.

Greatness is impossible to obtain or sustain in the comfort of pessimism.

Spend time today reflecting on your actions this week.

Did you meet the challenge? If not, why?

_____

_____

_____

_____

SUMMARY OF THE WEEK

YOUR THOUGHTS

BE AWARE OF WHAT YOU THINK

UNDERSTAND HOW YOUR THOUGHTS SHAPE YOUR REALITY

YOUR BEHAVIOR

BE MORE INTENTIONAL ABOUT THE DIRECTION YOU ALLOW YOUR MIND TO GO

THINK ABOUT IT

SPEAK ABOUT IT

BE ABOUT IT

 NEGATIVE THINKING TO POSITIVE THINKING

CHANGE
THE WAY YOU
THINK & SPEAK

What actions or behaviors can you and the people around you expect to see as a result of your change?

GREATNESS IS UPON YOU
CERTIFICATE OF COMPLETION

This is to certify that

_____

has successfully completed this week's challenge.

Eric Thomas and Associates, LLC

_____
signature

_____
date

WEEK 05

WORDS OF GREATNESS

PRESTIGE
reputation or influence arising from success, achievement, rank, or other favorable attributes

PURPOSE
the object to which one strives or to which one exists

GRASSHOPPER VS. ANT

Are you missing out on opportunities or taking advantage of what life brings you?

In the next two chapters, we are going to discuss why people miss out on opportunities and how you can make sure that you capitalize on every open window. This week, we discuss why there's no such thing as procrastination.

WEEK 05

"The key is not to prioritize what's on your schedule, but to schedule your priorities."

Stephen Covey

DEFINE THE PRIORITY

About 20 years ago, I had what could have possibly been the most game-changing opportunity of my life. By this time, I had finished undergrad and was fortunate enough to make, what I would eventually discover to be, lifelong friendships and associations. Among these friends were the Solomons. They were very successful doctors who propositioned me with a proposal. Apparently, they knew an engineer who had come up with an invention for special equipment that would help to drill oil, and they were in the process of getting it patented.

Mr. Solomon came to me because he knew that my speaking career was beginning to move and that I had just started to make a little bit of money; he apparently saw this as "An opportunity of a lifetime, my friend!", as he would often say.

I heard him out and, even though oil wells weren't my area of expertise, I believed it was a great idea and I wanted to invest in it. Unfortunately, a huge "BUT" task or event would inevitably get in the way of my being able to make the commitment:

- *"I want to invest BUT, I just booked a cruise..."*
- *"I want to invest BUT, I promised my..."*
- *"I want to invest BUT, we're starting a new program..."*
- *"I want to invest BUT, I've got a few other things to do first..."*

My plan was always to do it, it's just that I planned to do it <u>later</u>.

Months went by and they came back to me and asked me again, and I eventually told them that I couldn't make a move at that time. They warned me that this was the last opportunity to get in on the investment - I passed on it.

With just a ten-thousand dollar investment and a few years on the market, their invention made them millions of dollars - I was sick to my stomach.

That was the first opportunity I ever had to connect and grow with "movers and shakers" - people who not only had money but knew how to make it - and I didn't take advantage of it. From that day forward, I decided that I'll never let another opportunity come to me and not take advantage of it - you have to take advantage of an opportunity of a lifetime in the lifetime of the opportunity.

I learned a lot from my experience with the Solomons. What on earth could have caused me to miss out on that opportunity? Some would say procrastination. But I've learned that there's no such thing as procrastination (at least not in the way that most people use the word), it's more an issue of priority. All of the things I had going on at the time were legitimate, but my priorities were misaligned. I didn't miss out on an opportunity to take advantage of a million-dollar investment because I was lazy, disinterested, or unmotivated; it was because, as crazy as it sounds, the investment wasn't a number one priority for me.

DAY ONE: LEARN IT

To take advantage of an opportunity of a lifetime in the lifetime of the opportunity requires you to be able to set your priorities appropriately.

Take Advantage

Bottom line: you can't get to the top of the mountain by sitting in the valley. My experience with the Solomons is one of the most important lessons that I can teach. Everything I needed to become a millionaire at that time was right in front of me: I had the affluent circle of influence, the time, the energy, the money to invest in the project, and the trust of the people who propositioned me, but I didn't have a millionaire mindset... I didn't have the mindset needed to seize the moment. My priorities were misaligned.

Of an Opportunity of a Lifetime

> Some opportunities only come once in a lifetime

Some opportunities only come once in a lifetime, twice if you're lucky. These chances are unique because unlike the others, strategically taking advantage of them could mean that you have successfully altered your life's course far beyond measure.

Lebron James was put in this position when he had to choose between the Cleveland Cavaliers and the Miami Heat.

Merrill Lynch took his shot when he partnered with E.A. Pierce to bring "Wall Street to Main Street."

> To be Phenomenal, you have to be able to distinguish between everyday occurrences and one-shot moments.

Curtis Jackson, aka 50 Cent, took advantage of his opportunity when he decided to take equity in Glaceau for compensation for an endorsement deal instead of taking a salary.

To be Great, you have to be able to distinguish between everyday occurrences and one-shot moments.

In the Lifetime of the Opportunity

Have you ever noticed that the process of shopping for milk is different from the process of shopping for almost any other goods in the store? I thought about this one day when my wife texted me to remind me to pick up a gallon before I came home one night. <<*Make sure you pay attention to the expiration date this time!*>> she joked. <<*No doubt...,*>> I replied.

Everyone has done it: you go to the store and look for the refrigerator section; you glance at the different brands and prices; you look at the dates of all the cartons in the front row, and then you reach to the back and grab one of the cartons from the back of the row. Why do we do this? Because we know that the latest

> There are certain opportunities that have an expiration date on them and the longer it takes for you to make a move, the closer you are to letting it spoil.

expiration date will put us in the best position to get the most out of the milk. Sometimes, if you are diligent and consistent, you use all the milk before the expiration date. Other times, in spite of your efforts, you still open the refrigerator to a half carton of spoiled milk. Either way, everything about the way milk is sold, how it makes it into your refrigerator, and the urgency in which we make use of it says that it has its own priority (i.e., the expiration date, the rush to get it out of the car and into the fridge, etc.).

> But what I discovered was that my issue wasn't laziness or the uncontrollable urge to put things off until the last minute, it was simply that I would only make time to do those things that were truly important to me.

A similar concept applies to your opportunities. There are certain opportunities that have an expiration date on them, and the longer it takes for you to make a move, the closer you are to letting it spoil.

What major opportunities do you have sitting in the balance?

Why haven't you taken advantage of them?

> Its not that you can't get things done - it's that you can't get the most important things done within the time frame that they need to be done in.

Answer these questions in your Success Journal.

DAY TWO: ACCEPT IT

When I was younger, people would always tell me that I was a procrastinator. Since I didn't know any better, I embraced what they would tell me as truth. But what I discovered was that my issue wasn't laziness or the uncontrollable urge to put things off until the last minute, it was simply that I would only make time to do those things that were truly important to me. If it wasn't important to me, it would either never get done or it would get done at the latest possible moment. I never showed up late for football practice or social activities. I never showed up late to work on the day my pay-check was ready. And I never waited longer than a week to buy the latest album of my favorite group. I wasn't procrastinating... my priorities were misaligned. This is the challenge for many people. It's not that you can't get things done - it's that you can't get the most important things done within the time frame that they need to be done in.

> Remember, procrastination isn't about doing nothing until the last minute, it's about doing everything else you possibly can that's important to you before you do the activity that is being requested.

In your Journal, list the "Things that are Important to You" in column A and the "Things that are Expected of You, but aren't Important to You" in column B.

IMPORTANT TO YOU	EXPECTED OF YOU

On the balance beam below, list those things from columns A and B above that you spend most of your time doing on the left. Then list those things that you don't spend as much time doing from columns A and B on the right side of the balance beam. Are you spending more time doing things that are important to you or things that are not important to you but expected of you?

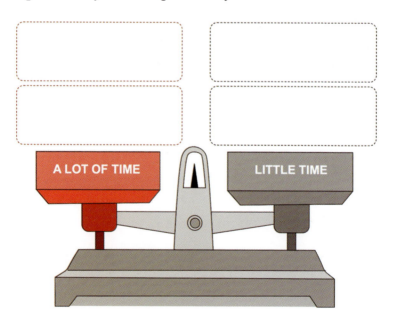

DAY THREE: EMBRACE IT

There was a time in my life when if I couldn't see the personal benefit or the urgency in it, chances were that, it wasn't important enough to me to get done right away. For example, I couldn't see the benefit in pursuing the Solomons' investment right away, even though doing so would have eventually led me to financial success. Other examples exist:

Students often don't see the immediate value in education and so class isn't a priority. As such, they may invest more time in extracurricular activities, hobbies, or other things of interest to them and teachers may erroneously view them as lazy.

In the corporate arena, projects are turned in at the last minute and deadlines are often missed because the employee didn't see the level of importance in it compared to his or her other responsibilities on the job. As such, the person may be viewed by his or her boss as being unmotivated.

Remember, procrastination isn't about doing nothing until the last minute, it's about doing everything else you possibly can that's important to you before you do the activity that is being requested.

In my training sessions, I tell my clients who struggle in this area to arrange all of the things that they have on their plate according to the following criteria:

- Not Important

- Important
- Very Important
- Emergency

This is a major step in learning how to prioritize your responsibilities and your goals.

- **Emergency** - has to be done within hours; it's a range between immediately and within that day (Short Period Expiration Date)
- **Very Important** - these things have to be done between 24hrs and 48hrs
- **Important** - important tasks have to be done within 3-4 days
- **Not Important -** you can decide the time frame that you are going to do these things but you have more than enough time to get them done (No Expiration Date)

What do you have going on in your life? Today, make a list of all your goals or make a list of all your responsibilities, and prioritize them according to the scale above. More space is provided in your Journal.

Goals, Responsibilities, and Priorities

_____

_____

_____

_____

_____

DAY FOUR: CHANGE IT

Begin with today in mind. Yesterday, you prioritized all of your goals and /or responsibilities. Today, prioritize all of your activities for today in order of **Emergency** to **Not Important** and complete activities from your list in the order of importance.

EMERGENCY	❏ ❏ ❏
VERY IMPORTANT	❏ ❏ ❏
IMPORTANT	❏ ❏ ❏
NOT IMPORTANT	❏ ❏ ❏

DAY FIVE: LIVE IT

Create a 7-day plan to take advantage of all of your opportunities.

SUNDAY   *i.e., Write my 7-day plan ...*
_____

*Use your GIUY Success Journal to write out your plan.

Greatness Is...

There is a fable that I used to hear when I was a kid about the grasshopper and the ant. In the story, the grasshopper sees a group of ants carrying kernels of corn and wants to know what they're getting ready to do with them. When one ant, too busy to talk, tells him that they're taking the kernels to their hill to store food for the winter, the grasshopper wanted to sing and play music instead. By the end of the fable, the winter weather comes, and the grasshopper is left hungry and unprepared.

My teacher would tell us this story to illustrate the importance of hard work and the evils of procrastination. To me, the issue for the grasshopper was never that he didn't want to prepare for the winter; it was that at the time when the opportunity was presented to him, there was something else that was more important to him, and he took for granted that the window to gather food would be available to him when he was ready to return to it. He made the mistake that we all are guilty of making at some point in our life - he underestimated the life span of the opportunity.

You will never be successful if you don't learn how to recognize those moments in your life that require you to make an immediate move.

Consider this: who were you supposed to be by now? CEO of your company? A college graduate? A lawyer? A leader in your community? Financially independent? How many life changing moments have you already let pass you by?

The grasshopper was bigger, stronger, and possibly faster, but he starved that winter. Why? Because he was ignorant to the value of what sacrificing something that he really wanted in that moment would bring to him in the future.

Because opportunities have a time frame, you can be stronger, smarter, and more passionate than the competition and still not make it to where you're supposed to be, because you never learned how to properly align your priorities.

Greatness is acquiring a sense of what is necessary to prepare you for the life you were meant to live.

Spend time today reflecting on your actions this week.

Did you meet the challenge? If not, why?

SUMMARY OF THE WEEK

WHAT MAJOR OPPORTUNITY DO YOU HAVE IN THE BALANCE?

CERTAIN OPPORTUNITIES HAVE AN EXPIRATION DATE

THE LONGER IT TAKES FOR YOU TO MAKE A MOVE, THE CLOSER YOU ARE TO LETTING IT SPOIL.

Are you spending more time doing things that are **IMPORTANT TO YOU**

or things that are not important to you?

EXPECTED OF YOU

PRIORITIZE ALL YOUR GOALS AND RESPONSIBILITIES

EMERGENCY — VERY IMPORTANT — IMPORTANT — NOT IMPORTANT

GREATNESS IS UPON YOU
CERTIFICATE OF COMPLETION

This is to certify that

_____

has successfully completed this week's challenge.

Eric Thomas and Associates, LLC

_____
signature

_____
date

WEEK **06**

WORDS OF GREATNESS

OPTIMIZE
to make the best or most effective use of

MINIMIZE VS. OPTIMIZE

Are you squeezing everything you can get out of the opportunities you're taking advantage of or are you leaving behind residual opportunities?

Last week we discussed the importance of taking advantage of the opportunity of a lifetime in the lifetime of the opportunity, but what do you do once you've made your move? This chapter focuses on how to get the most out of the opportunities you want to take advantage of.

WEEK 06

"I want to live my life so that my nights aren't full of regrets."

D.H. Lawrence

OPTIMIZE YOUR OPPORTUNITIES

How do you effectively take advantage of an opportunity? In the previous chapter, we talked about taking advantage of your opportunities, because some opportunities are only available to you for a limited amount of time. But once you've taken those necessary first steps in the right direction, how do you make your efforts, time, and money spent as effectively as possible?

One of the biggest challenges I've had in my speaking career, during peak traveling seasons, was working on the road. Somehow, something would always go wrong or end up missing. For instance, years ago, I would get on a plane after a long day of speaking and traveling and be ready to do some writing, but then I'd realize that all I have on me is my iPad, and the information I needed to access would be at home or in the office on my laptop. Or I would have both my iPad and my laptop, but the inconvenience of having to carry around both would ultimately make me choose one over the other, and I would always end up missing the one I left behind.

Then one night my Media Director, Karl, said, "E, you really need to optimize your iPad." He explained that if I backed all of my data up on the iCloud, it would be possible to sync my laptop and my iPad so the information that I had on one would always be on the other. For me, this was life-changing information, because it made it possible for me to not only take advantage of being able to do work while I'm on the road, but now I could work as effectively as possible.

> Short-cuts are only beneficial when they effectively help you to reach your goals.

Opportunities aren't immortal and, because the life span of any opportunity is unknown, you have to not only be willing to invest, you have to have a plan that will maximize the results within the time frame that you've been given. If you could be more, see more, have more... what would it look like? How can you use the momentum you currently have to get it?

DAY ONE: LEARN IT

No matter what the life span of each opportunity may be, you have to commit to finding the most effective way to not just pursue opportunities but get the most from them. Short-cuts are only beneficial when they effectively help you to reach your goals.

Less than five years ago, I was presented with the opportunity to create a vehicle to send inspirational and motivational messages to people across the world. I decided to take it and so Karl and I began taping our YouTube segment, "Thank God It's Monday!" in my backyard in the snow. We would stay up hours editing and re-editing to get the best quality motivational video on

YouTube every Monday. Less than five years later, I was filming TGIMs in Egypt, the UK, and Bermuda.

Less than five years ago, I was averaging 2-3 speaking gigs a month (most of which I didn't get paid for). But I gave every single gig everything I had. I treated the paid gigs the same way I treated the unpaid ones. Now, less than 5 years later, I'm speaking internationally, to corporations, colleges and universities, NFL, NBA, and MLB teams.

> The path from below average to becoming Great is going to require you to optimize every opportunity.

What am I trying to say? I'm telling you that investments are good, but it's not enough. In the span of 5 years, I went form filming in my backyard to filming in Cairo. And while I took advantage of the opportunities that were presented to me, the catalyst of my success was not my investment. It was my leverage.

I understood that my investment would get me paid gigs. I understood that my investment would change lives on a local level. I understood that my investment would open doors in certain circles; but to increase the potential return of my investment, I had to optimize every possible moment.

It wasn't enough to have the TGIMs on YouTube, I had to take the material, separate them into seasons and package them. It wasn't enough to tell my story from a podium, I had to write and publish it in a book. It wasn't enough to rely on friends and colleagues to put in a good word for me so that I can secure the next gig, I had to develop a team and we had to develop a plan. Together, we created a vehicle that made it possible for millions of people across the globe to be inspired and grow professionally on a daily basis.

The path from below average to becoming Great is going to require you to optimize every opportunity.

Are you getting the most out of every opportunity you're investing in?

> Ignorance, Confidence, and an Inability to Forecast are the three common obstacles that cause us to miss out on getting the most out of our opportunities.

DAY TWO: ACCEPT IT

Ignorance, Confidence, and an Inability to Forecast are the three common obstacles that cause us to miss out on getting the most out of our opportunities.

Ignorance

Ignorance - Sometimes we miss out on getting the most out of opportunities simply because we aren't aware or lack knowledge about what's available to us, because we were never taught (i.e., not knowing that my iPad and laptop could be synced hindered my productivity).

Confidence

Confidence - Sometimes we miss out on getting the most out of opportunities because we aren't confident in our ability to execute or perform (Imagine where Curtis Jackson, aka 50 cent, would be today if he didn't believe that he would be able to successfully fulfill his endorsement).

Inability to Forecast

> Acceptance is one of the most difficult parts of growth, but without it you'll never move beyond Average.

Inability to Forecast - Some of us miss out on getting the most out of opportunities because we have an inability to forecast future outcomes. (If Merrill Lynch didn't see the benefit in servicing smaller accounts, would his outcome have been the same?)

Acceptance is one of the most difficult parts of growth, but without it you'll never move beyond Average. Which of these reasons are getting in the way of you being able to get the most out of every opportunity?

	YES	SOMETIMES	NO
IGNORANCE			
CONFIDENCE			
PROCRASTINATION			

DAY THREE: EMBRACE IT

How long is it going to be ok to not know?

Now that you know at least three different obstacles that get in the way of you being able to capitalize on every opportunity, address your reason for why you have been ignorant, lacked confidence, and/or unable to forecast for so long.

DAY FOUR: CHANGE IT

The tragedy is not that you were ignorant, lacked confidence, or couldn't forecast. The tragedy begins when you know these things and choose to do nothing about them. Change can begin today. Optimizing every opportunity isn't easy, but it is simple. Here are a few things you can do to get the process started:

> Optimizing every opportunity isn't easy but it is simple.

- Share what you're doing with others. You never know who you'll talk to that can help you take your game to the next level.
- Take a chance. If that doesn't work out, take another chance. Failure is a part of the process, learn to embrace it and move on.
- Get over yourself. No one knows everything - including you. This brings me to #4:
- Ask questions. Who, What, When, and How are your life lines, know when to call them.
- No days off. I'm not telling you to not get any sleep or to work yourself into a coma, but what I am telling you is that if you start it, finish it.

CHALLENGE

What changes do you need to make to overcome the obstacles that you identified yesterday?

_____
_____
_____
_____

Share your idea with a friend or mentor to gain a different perspective.

DAY FIVE: LIVE IT

You can use this week to practice the changes that you listed yesterday. Create a 7-day plan to take advantage of all of your opportunities.

SUNDAY   *i.e., Write my 7-day plan ...*
_____

_____

*Use your GIUY Success Journal to write out your plan.

GREATNESS IS...

Candy Crush Saga will probably go down in history as one of the most popular social games to ever be developed. Today, it averages over 40 million users a month and is played over 600 million times a day. I can't get on a plane or walk into a building without either hearing someone talk about it or seeing someone playing it on their cell phone. I think the word that best describes it is: addictive.

King is the casual-social games company that developed Candy Crush Saga; and what I love about King is that the company illustrates what happens when you optimize an opportunity. King started with only a handful of entrepreneurs and, ten years later, it has one of the highest grossing social games to ever exist. The company revolutionized the game industry by going one step further than its competition - King made it possible for people to play their game across multiple platforms and still keep their place. Meaning, if you start playing on Facebook you could pick up where you left off on your mobile device.

King could have been content with just having Candy Crush be like any other multi-platform game but the company optimized what users would be able to do with it and in turn guaranteed its success.

It's not enough to just take advantage of an opportunity. What happens after you take the job offer? What's the next step after writing your book or paying for studio time to record your single? How many new steps can be created from your first step?

Greatness is exhausting every possibility from each opportunity.

Spend time today reflecting on your actions this week.

Did you meet the challenge? If not, why?

_____

_____

_____

SUMMARY OF THE WEEK

ARE YOU GETTING THE MOST OUT OF EVERY OPPORTUNITY YOU'RE INVESTESTING IN ?

3 COMMON OBSTACLES
that cause us to miss out on getting the most out of our opportunities

- IGNORANCE
- CONFIDENCE
- INABILITY TO FORECAST

ACCEPTANCE
the most difficult part of growth

What changes do you need to make to overcome the obstacles that you identified

MOVE BEYOND AVERAGE

GREATNESS IS UPON YOU
CERTIFICATE OF COMPLETION

This is to certify that

_____

has successfully completed this week's challenge.

Eric Thomas and Associates, LLC

_____
signature

_____
date

WEEK 07

WORDS OF GREATNESS

COMPETITION

the effort of two or more parties acting independently to secure the business of a third party by offering the most favorable terms

UNDER COMPETITION VS. COMPETITIVE EDGE

Do you step into the ring prepared for the fight or prepared for the win?

In this chapter we discuss the significance of knowing your competition and how vision and planning play into your ability to gain a competitive edge.

WEEK 07

"We all want to be the best at something. Trouble is, some people are only the best at being second best."

- Jarod Kintz

BE SMARTER THAN THE COMPETITION

"This will be the biggest upset since Sonny Liston...I'm the underdog, if he hits me I'm in trouble like the Sonny Liston fight. But I came back and I shook the world when I got Liston ... [now] I'm meeting another big bad strong monster - a knockout artist that beats everybody...George Foreman knocked out Norton...Frasier ... [but] I'm so fast...so scientific...listen, if you think the world was surprised when Nixon resigned, wait 'till I whip Foreman's behind."

- Muhammad Ali quote from "Rumble in the Jungle" interview

I was watching some old footage of the "Rumble in the Jungle" interview, and its still crazy to me that a dethroned Muhammad Ali had just gotten reinstated to fight, and he comes back into the ring three years later to fight the current heavy-weight champ, George Foreman, who was significantly younger than him and in the prime of his career. You couldn't create a more alluring underdog and, though the odds were against him, he knew that the only way he could win was that he had to have a competitive edge... he wasn't as fast anymore, he wasn't as young, and he had been defeated twice after reentering the ring by Norton and Frasier who both were defeated by Foreman. If Ali was going to fight with a giant, then he had to have a plan. The rope-a-dope was Ali's competitive edge.

I believe the Foreman vs. Ali match is not only one of the greatest boxing matches of all times, it's also one of the greatest illustrations of a life-changing message: you don't have to be faster than your competition, you don't even have to be stronger; but you must be smarter if you plan to get ahead.

Many believe that the rope-a-dope method was merely a defense mechanism used by Ali to detract from the effects of Foreman's powerful blows. However, when you take a step back and really look at the fight and listen to what both of the fighters were saying during the post fight interviews, both fighters reveal that the rope-a-dope was more than a means to drain Foreman of his energy, Ali went into the ring planning to have a competitive edge.

In the match, Ali's eyes were always on Foreman, he knew exactly what was coming and put himself in the best position to offset Foreman's rhythm. He was able to successfully stop Foreman's momentum physically, by gaining head control so that he didn't get hit. And then to top it off, he got into Foreman's head by whispering in his ear, "They told me you could punch... is that all you've got?" This threw Foreman off of his game.

Ali's competitive edge was both physical and mental head control, and though by Ali's own admission, Foreman's punches were killing him, instead of showing his competition his pain, he used it to his advantage.

Having a competitive edge separated the great from the Greatest.

DAY ONE: LEARN IT

"When you're fighting a Mummy, you keep a step ahead of the Mummy... I shall be the Mummy's curse that night."

-Muhammad Ali

to be Great, you must plan with a vision in mind.

Vision. I loved the interview that Ali had before his fight with Foreman. Aside from it being hilarious, it illustrated one fundamental point that's necessary for achieving Greatness: to be Great, you must plan with a vision in mind. From the interview, you can tell that Ali saw himself as the Greatest - his vision was to claim ownership of the World Champion title. When he got in the ring, his strategy, while important, was just a means to an anticipated end. The world is full of people who constantly try to duplicate or expand upon the strategies of others and fail - not because it wasn't a good strategy, but because they failed to see or understand the vision.

the further away you get from the vision, the less impactful the plan.

Corporations have this challenge all the time when their founding partners have died or retired. They find that their companies operate at peak levels as long as the founders or visionaries are behind the wheel, but sales, profits, and productivity dwindle when they're gone. This phenomenon occurs because the further away you get from the vision, the less impactful the plan.

What vision do you have in mind when you think about going up against your competitor?

DAY TWO: ACCEPT IT

There is a difference between your perceived competitors and your real competitors, and you want to know the difference because your real competitors may have traits that you have yet to master. They are the ones who you need to stay ahead of.

Prepare a "Competitors' List." Identify your perceived competitors - people who are in a similar field and your real competitors - people who are actually doing what you are doing.

> You've got to know how many steps your competitors are ahead of you.

What's your vision when it comes to competing with them?

_____

_____

_____

DAY THREE: EMBRACE IT

What's your plan? You can't just "wing it" to Greatness. You have to have a strategy to get a jump on your competitors.

The Art of War, by Sun Tzu, places emphasis on the importance of strategy in warfare and knowing your competition. You've got to know how many steps your competitors are ahead of you. You have to be precise and strategic to win the war!

One of the things I learned from a fighter who I mentored a while back that was impressive, is that he studied and understood the strengths of his competitors - he learned their strengths and weaknesses and developed a counter attack for each of their attacks. He altered his fighting style every match so that he could triumph over his competition.

> Average people develop a plan and stick with it even when it's obvious that it isn't working.

Now that you know who your competitor is, research and identify what strategies your competitors use to make them successful.

_____

_____

_____

_____

DAY FOUR: CHANGE IT

Remember, having a vision is half the battle, strategizing is the other half. Knowing what to do first and the sequence is critical to staying ahead of your competitors, and you have to know when a plan is working for you and when it's working against you. I learned that lesson the hard way during the early stages of our company through our shipping process. We sold the first 5,000 copies of *The Secret to Success* without a concrete shipping structure. Our plan was to figure out the best shipping structure as we went along through trial and error. In truth, we should have had the shipping infrastructure in place before we started selling books. Not having this structure caused a lot of shipping errors on our part - and a lot of unhappy customers. In the world of business, even one unhappy customer gives the competition a competitive edge. This is a lesson learned for me and my team and because of it, I can't emphasize the importance of having a strategy enough. After some thorough research of the shipping structure of other companies (our competitors), we developed a system that works better for us and we managed to minimize customer complaints exponentially. Average people develop a plan and stick with it even when its obvious that it isn't working.

Now that you have identified your competitor's success traits, determine which ones you need to incorporate and develop a strategy for how you will use this information to defeat your competition.

_____

_____

_____

DAY FIVE: LIVE IT

Now that you've identified your competition and your missing success traits, it's time to EXECUTE. Create a 7-day plan to describe what you will do to get ahead of the competition.

SUNDAY   *i.e., Write my 7-day plan ...*_____

_____

*Use your GIUY Success Journal to write out your plan.

GREATNESS IS...

Howard Cosell said, "The ultimate victory in competition is derived from the inner satisfaction of knowing that you have done your best and that you have gotten the most out of what you had to give."

Listen, everybody has something special that they can bring to the table - a unique skill, creative energy, organization, well adapted social skills, etc. One of the greatest human attributes is our ability to be and express our uniqueness. But because we are all unique in our own rights, if you're looking to get ahead and stay ahead of your competition, you have to be willing to run that extra mile. You have to be willing to do what the next man wouldn't or couldn't because he was too distracted.

You can make it through the finish line; you can make it to the head of your class; you can become the new VP or COO of your company; you can manage your department; you can take your team to the playoffs; you can run circles around all of your competition, whomever they may be- but you've got to come to the table prepared.

The victory in competition isn't knowing that you won. Its knowing that when you were sitting at the table amongst the Greats, that you exhausted your talents and strengths to become the Greatest.

Greatness is realizing that the dividing line between you and your competition is how prepared you came to fight.

Spend time today reflecting on your actions this week.

Did you meet the challenge? If not, why?

_____

_____

_____

SUMMARY OF THE WEEK

KNOW THE DIFFERENCE BETWEEN REAL AND PERCEIVED COMPETITORS,
PREPARE A COMPETITORS LIST

YOU'VE GOT TO KNOW HOW MANY STEPS YOUR COMPETITORS ARE AHEAD OF YOU
You have to be precise and strategic to win the war!

WHAT'S YOUR PLAN ?

What vision do you have in mind when you think about going up against your competitor?

TO BE PHENOMENAL, YOU MUST PLAN WITH A VISION IN MIND

Now that you know who your competitor is, research and identify what strategies your competitors use to make them successful.

having a vision is half the battle, strategizing is the other half.

GREATNESS IS UPON YOU
CERTIFICATE OF COMPLETION

This is to certify that

_____

has successfully completed this week's challenge.

Eric Thomas and Associates, LLC

_____
signature

_____
date

WEEK

08

WORDS OF GREATNESS

CURRENCY
something that is used as a medium of exchange; general acceptance

LEGACY
heritage

SERVICE
an act of helpful activity

CURRENCY VS. LEGACY

Do you gauge success by how much money you obtain or by how many people you've managed to influence while you lived?

The next three chapters will discuss different aspects of service and its significance to your ability to obtain Greatness in all aspects of life. This week, we will focus on establishing longevity by investing in the lives of others.

WEEK 08

"When you get to a place where you don't live for what you can get, but you live for what you can give, you will see your life change tremendously."

Unknown

A LIFE OF SACRIFICE

"I don't want to go! Mommy, no!" Cadence screamed, struggling to break free of the officer's grip of her wrist, "Where are they taking us? I want to stay with my mommy!"

Loretta broke away from the tiny hands of her younger children, desperately holding on to her in an attempt to reach for Cadence as the officer was pulling her away, only to be intercepted by the other officer who had been standing, silent and rigid in judgment the whole time he was on her front porch.

"Loretta," the case worker whispered, as though the subtleness of her tone would somehow quiet the tumultuous scene. "Loretta, you're making this harder than it has to be. When you clean yourself up and prove to the court that you can handle having your children back in your custody, your family can be together again." Cadence could hear the conversation that the case worker was having with her mother from the car.

Of the thousands of things that went through her mind as she rode away staring at her mom through the back window of the navy blue Lincoln Town Car, she remembered thinking three things:

1) She had to make her way back to her mom;

2) She had to finish school; and

3) She had to save her family.

At the case worker's request, Cadence turned around in her seat and buckled her seat belt. As she reached over to help her younger brother who was struggling with his belt, she was haunted by a final thought: *how does a poor black girl from 7 Mile and Woodward in Detroit, Michigan even begin to dream of making a better life for herself and her family?*

Even as a child, Cadence knew that money wasn't everything. She had seen too many people have it and spend it and die miserable. And even if she were to make it through high school, no one in her family had ever made it to college.

She knew things could be different. She knew that she was different. But how could she prove this to the world? How could she help her family? What kind of legacy would she be able to leave?

DAY ONE: LEARN IT

Today, there are some circles that debate over who is more likely to be remembered 50 years from now: Steve Jobs or Bill Gates. Both are known for their entrepreneurial genius - Microsoft and Apple are household names. While I don't have the answer for who will be remembered longer, I believe that Bill Gates has accomplished that which many other entrepreneurs continue to struggle with - learning the difference between Legacy and Currency. Everybody knows that Bill Gates and money are practically synonymous; he's one of the wealthiest men in the world, and people joke and say that if he were to drop a $100 bill that he wouldn't even bend over to pick it up. But what I admire about Gates is that he walked away from a career that placed him at the top of the list of the world's wealthiest people on the planet and instead focused his attention on pouring into the American Education System. As a matter of fact, he gave special attention to disadvantaged students - those kids who, because of their economic backgrounds, would potentially have more of a challenge in obtaining success.

Through his philanthropy, Gates has given other people the opportunity to create currency and legacies of their own. This is exactly what he did for Cadence. He gave a poor girl from Detroit an opportunity to make good on a promise she made when she was in the back seat of that Lincoln Town Car.

By the start of her senior year, Cadence was already accepted into several colleges but had no way of paying tuition. But then her guidance counselor told her about "The Gates Millennium Scholarship" - a full ride scholarship awarded to 1,000 of the top high school students in the country in need of financial support. Like many students at that time, Cadence knew nothing about Bill Gates' scholarship foundation; all she knew was that he was an extremely wealthy man.

She told me about how rigorous the process was and how nerve wracking the waiting period had been. This was her opportunity to make a better life for her and her family. And then it happened:

"Dear Cadence McCastle, we are pleased to inform you that you have been awarded the Gates Millennium Scholarship!"

One of 1,000 that year, Cadence's life began to change.

> Contrary to what Average people believe, wealth is not the equivalent of success, longevity is.

Today, Cadence is a graduate of Michigan State University and has successfully moved her family away from 7 Mile and Woodward in Detroit, Michigan. Cadence will always remember Bill Gates and how his scholarship fund changed her life. He not only gave her an opportunity to move beyond her means financially, but he also gave her an opportunity to create a legacy of her own - she was a first generation college graduate and now her siblings are in college as well. Contrary to what average people believe, wealth is not the equivalent of success, longevity is.

What is the purpose of success without significance? I know we don't usually think about it while we're making it, but it's true nonetheless, you can't take money with you when you die - bottom line.

You can't take your tax bracket, your social status, or your elite standing with you when your time on earth has expired. But the impact and influence you've made on other people's lives is an investment that will last forever.

This is what adds significance to success - the marked difference between currency and legacy. Currency blesses the individual. Legacy is taking that currency and blessing others.

Are you building a legacy or merely collecting currency?

DAY TWO: ACCEPT IT

> Currency blesses the individual. Legacy is taking that currency and blessing others.

My personal experiences make me so adamant about this. I've lived investing in others, and the return on my investment far exceeds anything I could ever have reaped from investing in my personal interests alone or merely seeking monetary gain. In 1992, I started the GED class for high school dropouts, and 5 years later I started my first non-profit organization, Break the Cycle I Dare You, whose mission was to break the cycle of crime, hopelessness, and despair to all it reached. In 2005, I started the Advantage, a retention program for minorities at Michigan State University. Then I began the TGIM series in hopes that people would find the series as a source of inspiration on YouTube, and as a result of focusing on changing the lives of others, my life changed forever. If you want to be successful in life, you've got to shift from it always being about you and start allowing it to be about others. Life has a way of giving back to you what you allow yourself to give to it.

Think about a person, group of people, or organization that you can invest some time and energy in. If necessary, research some different causes online or come up with a cause, organization, or non-profit of your own. For example, consider doing some volunteer work for a group home in your neighborhood, the Boys and Girls Club, Red Cross, or some other charitable organization. What can you do to make your time on earth memorable?

DAY THREE: EMBRACE IT

One of my favorite movies is, *Pay It Forward* because it illustrates selflessness in a way that most people struggle with. I had my team watch this movie together and make a note of the RANDOM ACTS of KINDNESS. Watch this movie or another movie with a similar theme with your company, students, or organization. What can you do to change the life of someone else with one simple act of kindness?

DAY FOUR: CHANGE IT

Making the shift from currency to legacy can begin as early as today. A strong legacy can be created even when you don't have a dime to your name. Sometimes we can get so preoccupied with life that we don't realize how our actions or inactions not only affect us economically but beyond the grave as well.

How do you create a legacy?

Vision

We discussed vision as it relates to getting a jump on your competitors in a previous chapter. But having a vision is equally important when trying to create a legacy. Consider what you are most passionate about. What can you do to position yourself to be able to pour into that passion on a daily basis while helping other people? What do you want to be remembered for?

Strategy/Plan

How do you make your vision a reality? Who is involved? What will you need to get it going?

Build the Foundation

The truth is, everyone has something that they'll be remembered for, but that's not necessarily a good thing. You want to make sure that you're leaving behind something of value and, to do this, you must build your character. *Revisit Week One.*

Accountability

Tell people about what you're doing and ask them to check in with you periodically. This is a good practice, even if it's only to remind you of the promises you made yourself.

What is the one thing that you can do today to begin your legacy?

DAY FIVE: LIVE IT

Now that you know how to get started, create a 7-day plan to develop a legacy for yourself using the tools from Day Four.

SUNDAY   *i.e., Write my 7-day plan ...*
_____

_____

*Use your GIUY Success Journal to write out your plan.

GREATNESS IS...

Marian Wright Edelman, President of the Children's Defense Fund said, "Never work just for money or for power. They won't save your soul or help you sleep at night."

Success is selfish. Just because you're successful doesn't mean that you're significant. Money does make you rich, but rich people die everyday failing to make a significant impact on the lives of the people who they had the chance to touch. The reality is that money, though necessary in many regards, is easily acquired and more easily spent. For this reason, there will always be somebody more educated, with more possessions and more money, to take their place. But when you're significant, people will always keep a place open for you. Mother Teresa, Martin Luther King Jr., and Ghandi may not have been business tycoons, but they were rich in what they gave because they enhanced the lives of others. Investing in the lives of others not only establishes longevity, it creates significance.

What will the headlines of the obituary say when it's your time to leave?

Greatness is not taking for granted the lasting impact that giving to others can have on not just your life, but the lives of those you invested in.

Spend time today reflecting on your actions this week.

Did you meet the challenge? If not, why?

_____

_____

_____

_____

SUMMARY OF THE WEEK

CURRENCY — the money you make

LEGACY — leaving a mark after you die

ARE YOU BUILDING A LEGACY OR COLLECTING CURRENCY?

INVEST YOUR TIME **AND** YOUR ENERGY

ON A PERSON, A GROUP OF PEOPLE, OR AN ORGANIZATION

PERFORM A RANDOM ACT OF **KINDNESS**

What is the one thing that you can do today to begin your legacy?

HOW DO YOU CREATE A LEGACY ?

VISION - STRATEGY - FOUNDATION - ACCOUNTABILITY

GREATNESS IS UPON YOU
CERTIFICATE OF COMPLETION

This is to certify that

_____

has successfully completed this week's challenge.

Eric Thomas and Associates, LLC

_____
signature

_____
date

WEEK 09

WORDS OF GREATNESS

RECIPROCITY
a mutual exchange

ALL ABOUT ME VS. RECIPROCITY

Do you live a life that says, "It's all about me" or does your life say, "I remember others"?

In the previous chapter, we discussed that currency is not the true measure of success - it's the impact you've had on others. Now, we will take a look at a more intimate type of service, one that requires you to do the remembering of others as opposed to doing things that will lead to others remembering you.

WEEK 09

"It isn't until you begin to fight in your own cause that you become really committed to winning, and become a genuine ally of other people struggling for their freedom."

Robin Morgan

BECOME A CHAMPION OF SERVICE

...I was on campus in a planning session for Bell Tower Ministries. What I wasn't doing was handling my responsibilities as a new husband. Until one evening, or should I say one early morning, I came home about 2 a.m. from the Bell Tower [meeting]. The Bell generally ended right at curfew, 10:30 p.m., but sometimes we would go to one of the dorms to do a follow-up session. This particular night we got into a deep discussion with the twins, Paul and Patrick, and afterwards we stopped by the Waffle House. When I walked in the house and eventually in the bedroom, Dee looked at me and started crying.

"What's wrong?" I asked as I sat next to her on the bed. I thought she was having some challenges in the nursing program, and that she was probably just a little frustrated because school was so demanding. "It's you," Dee said with an attitude.

"Me, what did I do?" I asked, confused. "I am out here trying to do my thing for the ministry."

"That's the problem, the ministry! Did you marry the ministry or me?"

"I married you," I responded quickly.

"Act like it then! You spend all your time on campus or with your boys while I sit here waiting for you to come home.

[Passage from The Secret to Success *by Eric Thomas.]*

Lauryn Hill said it best when she asked, "Who do I have to be to get some reciprocity?" That's exactly what my wife was asking when we had that conversation about Bell Tower over 20 years ago, and I haven't been the same since.

I can't tell you how important it is to pour back into others what they have poured into you. In the previous chapter, we talked about the importance of creating a legacy. Remember, true success extends beyond monetary gain and is dependent on your ability to invest in others and make their dreams come true. But in this chapter, we explore another form of service - reciprocity. Many times, it's easier to show kindness to strangers - there's no history and no emotional attachments. But our family and friends we often take for granted, especially the ones who are closest to us. And trust me, I know how easy it is to get caught up in your studies, career, and just life in general, but it is imperative to never forget your family and friends who supported and still support you along the way. My wife was there for me when I had nothing. She was there for me emotionally, and she was there for me spiritually. She was, and is to this day, my best friend. When I was homeless and sleeping in abandoned buildings, she made sure that I had something to eat. She had every right to feel the way that she did that night.

Don't just spend time seeking your own success or motivating and gaining inspiration for yourself; you increase your significance when you remember those who helped you get the process started.

DAY ONE: LEARN IT

I had a friend when I was younger, during one of the most difficult times of my life. He was responsible for bringing me into the church and, eventually, that led to me getting off of the streets. His actions put me in the position to meet the pastor who encouraged me to get my GED and wrote the letter of recommendation that got me into school.

> Reciprocity is a mutual exchange of benefits.

Unfortunately, when I went off to college, my friend stayed behind and eventually was overcome by some of the negative peer pressure in the city of Detroit; his life began to take a turn for the worse; and it tore me apart, because I knew that if it had not been for him leading me into that church, I would not be where I am today.

Reciprocity is a mutual exchange of benefits. My first few years in undergrad were spent thinking about my friend and the pastor back in Detroit, and I knew that no matter what happened to me at Oakwood that I had to make a return on their investment.

The pastor would never accept anything that I offered to him personally, but he told me that the way that I could repay him is by helping people the way that he helped me. And I have committed my life to trying to fulfill this mission through the GED program that I started years ago and several other service projects and initiatives that I've been active in since that time.

Perhaps there is someone in your life who recently lost his or her job who was responsible for helping you to start your dream career.

Maybe your mother and/or grandmother weren't fortunate enough to go to college but worked overtime to pay your tuition for school, because they wanted you to have a better chance than they did; and this chance ultimately positioned you to become that engineer, doctor, or lawyer you always dreamed of becoming.

Whoever these people are, give thoughtful consideration to how they helped you and think about how you can give them a return on their investment.

DAY TWO: ACCEPT IT

We get so busy pursuing, we often forget to reflect. It's not enough for you to just remember the people; what sacrifices did they make and how did you directly benefit from those sacrifices?

Even if you're not in a position to repay them directly (i.e., because they're deceased), you can still sew into others what that person sewed in to you.

Yesterday, you thought about at least one person who helped get you to where you are today. This person could have:

- helped your career;
- taken care of you when you were younger;
- provided you with food or shelter when you were experiencing difficult times;

- given you a shoulder to cry on when you needed it most; or
- mentored you in your field.

Reciprocity invites gratitude.

The list is endless. Today, I want you to write a "Thank You" letter to that person or those people who helped you. Even if you can't mail the letter off, write the letter anyway and thank that person for stepping up and lending a hand. Reciprocity invites gratitude.

DAY THREE: EMBRACE IT

Don't get greedy with the inspiration! Many times, to keep us pumped and lifted throughout the day or through a trial, we reach for motivational or inspirational messages or videos to help us. We might even thank others for sending them to us! But how often do you intentionally look for ways to inspire the people or person who lifted you up when you were down?

Reciprocity requires selfless inspiration even when you don't feel like it.

When was the last time you called your mom or dad just to give them something to help them through their day?

How often do you post or email an inspirational phrase or quote to your employee, boss, or a colleague who helped you meet your last deadline?

It's the little things that separate the Average from the Great. Reciprocity requires selfless inspiration even when you don't feel like it.

This morning, complete the following:

Today I commit to reaching out to

_____

I will share with him/her the following motivational message:

_____

_____

_____

Call and share with the person the reason you're sending the motivational message his or her way.

DAY FOUR: CHANGE IT

We're talking about reciprocity for one simple reason: people forget. It doesn't seem like a big deal when you're the one doing the forgetting, but what about the forgotten?

What is it about relationships that make them so easily severed?

Athletes divorce their high school sweethearts - women who have been in their corner for years, yet they become tied up in ugly divorces.

Professionals who made their way to the top, ignore interns and eager first-year college graduates, making it difficult for them to learn and get ahead.

...people forget

Teachers over-discipline their students, removing them from the classroom instead of working with them to make sure that they get some benefit from that day's lesson.

The reason that we are so willing and able to detach and drift away from certain people, groups, and memories is because we forget the investment. We forget that teachers were once patient and tolerant with us. We forget that we were once struggling after graduating from college and desperately needed a break. And we forget that girl who we sat next to in class; who helped with that paper and held your hand before the money and the fame.

What do you need to do to make sure that you are living a life that isn't all about you?

- **Remember.** Remember the ones who helped you get to where you are or where you're going; remember what it was like before you made it; and remember that you didn't get there on your own.
- Payback who you owe.

I went back for my friend in Detroit a few years into school. I got a summer job selling magazines and, instead of doing it myself, we sold the magazines together and split the profits. Eventually, he was able to move to Alabama with me and lived with me and my wife until he got back on his feet. I genuinely wanted to expose him to what he gave me: an opportunity to be exposed to by introducing me to that pastor.

Today can be the day that you take another step towards Greatness. This week you've discovered gratitude in reciprocity and selfless inspiration. Now you're going to do or give something tangible to someone who helped you when you were low.

The goal is to physically show that person in a concrete way your gratitude and to simply convey the message: I remember you.

DAY FIVE: LIVE IT

Create a 7-day plan that you can follow to give back to someone who helped you. This week you weren't able to get to everybody on that list, but who else do you need to reach out to? Be intentional about thinking about these people, and how you will reciprocate their investment.

SUNDAY   *i.e., Write my 7-day plan ...*
_____

_____

*Use your GIUY Success Journal to write out your plan.

GREATNESS IS...

There is a parable about a Samaritan who stopped to help a man who had been attacked by robbers who left him half dead. The Samaritan bandaged his wounds, gave him food and drink, and made sure he was taken care of until he recovered. What would it say about the guy who was robbed, at a time in his life where he was at his best, if he were to see the Samaritan, now wounded and down on his luck, and not do anything to help him?

We should never forget those people who provided for us when we couldn't provide for ourself. But worse than forgetting, is remembering and doing nothing about it. Why? Because it shows a weakness in character that can only be described as selfish. And selfishness doesn't sustain success - it destroys it.

You didn't get to where you are in life because you deserve it, you got there because someone thought enough of you to give you a chance. Someone said, "Yes, I'll look out for you." "Yes, I believe in you," "Yes, I'll give you what you need." "Yes, I'll be there when you call me."

Greatness is demonstrating humility in all aspects of life. If you can't reach back, you will never move forward.

Spend time today reflecting on your actions this week.

Did you meet the challenge? If not, why?

_____

_____

_____

_____

_____

SUMMARY OF THE WEEK

RECIPROCITY
A MUTUAL EXCHANGE OF SERVICE

Give thoughtful consideration to how the person helped you and think about how you can give them a return on their investment.

WRITE A "THANK YOU" LETTER

RECIPROCITY INVITES GRATITUDE

SONGS - POEMS - QUOTES - MOVIES - ETC.

SOURCES OF INSPIRATION

think of a person that you can call or visit this week
think about how you can pour into them today

SHARE YOUR INSPIRATIONS
LIFT THEIR SPIRIT

The goal is to physically show that person in a concrete way your gratitude and to simply convey the message: I remember you.

GREATNESS IS UPON YOU
CERTIFICATE OF COMPLETION

This is to certify that

_____

has successfully completed this week's challenge.

Eric Thomas and Associates, LLC

_____
signature

_____
date

WEEK

10

WORDS OF GREATNESS

ENTITLEMENT
to give (a person or thing) a title, right, or claim to something

ENTITLEMENT VS. LIFE OF SERVICE

Do you view life in terms of what people owe you or in terms of what you can give back to people?

So far, we've discussed two aspects of Service: giving back to the people or cause that was instrumental in getting you started and giving others an opportunity to benefit from your success. This week we will discuss the distinction between service and entitlement.

WEEK 10

"I don't got to...I get to."

Eric Thomas

I DON'T GOT TO, I GET TO...

« Meet me at the altar in your white dress. We ain't getting no younger so we might as well do it. You've been here all the while girl so I must confess...I just want to get married...baby let's get married. »

-Jagged Edge "Let's Get Married"

Life isn't as much about what happens to you as it is about your perspective. I married my wife, Dee, 23 years ago but we didn't have an actual ceremony until 21 years into our marriage. The first time we said our vows, we weren't in the position financially to have the dream wedding she wanted, and so we waited until we could do the ceremony debt free. I remember holding her hand the day we got married thinking, "Wow. I can't believe that she is going to be my wife." And on the day we renewed our vows, watching her walk down the aisle 21 years later, I thought to myself, "Wow. I can't believe this is my wife."

I get a lot of calls and invites from churches, companies, and couples to do marital counseling. Statistics currently show that an estimated 50% of all marriages end in divorce. I believe that the biggest divisive factor in most broken relationships (marriages and otherwise) is that people feel entitled. For most marriages, the time between the engagement period to a few years after the honeymoon marks the blissful stage. In this stage, the energy is high and there is a positive outlook on your ability to do everything and get through anything together.

But over the course of time, you start to notice things that somehow slid under the radar before. Those things that you found charming when you first got married, now annoy you. As it turns out, that's not her real eye color, that's not her real hair, his jokes aren't that funny, and you never noticed how much of a "Momma's Boy" he truly is. And even these "adjustments" would be ok, but what really damages a relationship is that as time moves on and you've made all of these adjustments and compromises, you begin to develop a sense of entitlement.

When people feel entitled, they tend to function in their relationship with a *"You owe me"* mindset instead of a *"How may I serve you?"* mindset.

You stop saying *"Thank you"* and *"Please."* And *"Sweetie, did you remember the orange juice?"* turns into *"How many times do I have to tell you that I don't like pulp?"* You become comfortable with being edgy, snappy, short, impatient, and judgmental. There is no love, joy, peace, kindness, or gentleness. Because you feel entitled, you act entitled. You act like it's your wife's responsibility to serve you. You act like your husband is supposed to cater to your every demand. It's not always obvious at first, but when you feel like you have a right to something, you're more into satisfying yourself than the other person; and your behavior says very loudly, "This is what you owe me", "I deserve this", and "I can do this if I want to."

The same thing happens when people get a new job. When it's fresh, you go to work early, you're there after-hours, you come in whenever they need you, you turn in reports and projects on time. But once you've been there for a while, you come in late, you disparage the company, you take longer lunch breaks, and you're logged in to Facebook all day.

> it is important to learn the difference between approaching life feeling like you're owed something and approaching it with a desire to serve selflessly.

On the other hand, when you live your life like someone who doesn't believe that he or she is owed something, your behavior says, "Let me help you", "I am grateful", and "I can't wait to be a part". In a marriage or any other relationship, there has to be a healthy amount of "give and take." But more important than the "taking" aspect is giving - not with the intent of receiving anything in return, but because you know in your heart that at any given moment anyone else could have been chosen to do what you're doing and, by grace, it gets to be you.

DAY ONE: LEARN IT

An entitlement refers to the belief that one has the right to a particular award or benefit.

In my work in the school system, I've seen the effects of the Entitlement mindset on our youth. So much is given to them freely from the time of their birth that they underestimate and under-appreciate the value in many of the things their parents and grandparents weren't allowed to take for granted.

Unfortunately, this mentality bleeds over into the workforce creating companies, organizations, and school districts that are full of employees who demand to get paid, but only partially meet the job requirements, show up to work when they want to, brown-nose, work in isolation, and the list goes on. The words "I'm proud to be an American" aren't as significant for them, because they are so far removed from the principles of hard work and sacrifice that helped to shape this country.

To progress, it is important to learn the difference between approaching life feeling like you're owed something and approaching it with a desire to serve selflessly.

Identify 5 areas in your life where you function as though you have an entitled mindset. Meaning, your behavior says that the company you work for, your teachers, or anyone who you are involved in any type of relationship with owes you some benefit or award.

1. _____
2. _____
3. _____
4. _____
5. _____

Identify 5 areas in your life where you function as though you have a mindset of service. Meaning, your behavior says that you are grateful and willing to do whatever is necessary to see a positive end result.

1. _____
2. _____
3. _____
4. _____
5. _____

DAY TWO: ACCEPT IT

The truth is that we all feel that we are owed something to some extent by at least one person in our life. And sometimes that debt is justified, but the question is, what side of the spectrum consumes more of your life? Do you live mostly with an attitude that says you are owed something or is your life a life filled with expressions of gratitude and service?

Yesterday, you identified areas in your life where you felt entitled and areas in your life where you expressed gratitude. Today, you are going to accept which behavior you identify more with when it comes to your approach in life.

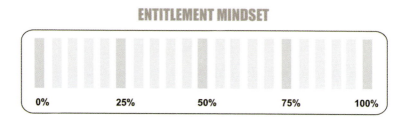

- 0% -I never feel like anyone owes me anything.

- 25%-I rarely feel like anyone owes me anything.
- 50%- I sometimes feel like I'm entitled to certain benefits or rewards.
- 75%- Many times, I feel like its my right to have certain benefits or rewards.
- 100% - I always feel like I'm entitled to certain benefits or rewards.

- 0%- I never behave in a spirit of gratitude and service to others.
- 25%- I rarely behave in a spirit of gratitude and service to others.
- 50% - I sometimes behave in a spirit of gratitude and service to others.
- 75%-Most times I behave in a spirit of gratitude and service to others.
- 100% - I always behave in a spirit of gratitude and service to others.

DAY THREE: EMBRACE IT

Today, you are going to get more specific about areas in your life where you feel a false sense of entitlement.

View a few of the examples below to get you moving in the right direction:

I expect to get paid on time every pay period even when I don't fully perform the duties of my job.

I expect to get good grades even when I don't put in the needed study time or meet with the teachers/professors.

I expect my significant other/friends to treat me with respect even when I don't treat them with the same respect.

On your own:

I expect _____

_____

even when I _____

_____

DAY FOUR: CHANGE IT

People who have a sense of entitlement often feel burdened when things don't go in their favor, and so they feel that they "got to do" and not that they "get to do" what they are doing.

"Got to do" - feel burdened, pressured, like you don't have a choice.

"Get to do" - feel honored, excited, grateful that you get a chance.

When you are unrestricted and grateful, you live life feeling excited and empowered, knowing that you "get to do" the things that you're doing.

List 3 things that you feel that you "got to do":

1. _____

2. _____

3. _____

What does your behavior look like in these situations? How do people respond to your behavior, and is that the response that will help you to live your fullest life?

_____

_____

_____

DAY FIVE: LIVE IT

Draft your 7-day plan to live a life that is based more on those things you "get to do" and not "got to do."

SUNDAY *i.e., Write my 7-day plan ...*

_____

*Use your GIUY Success Journal to write out your plan.

Greatness Is...

A while ago, someone emailed me a story about a little girl during the Depression. In the story, the little girl went to the store with her mom, and when they walked out of the store and walked up the street a few blocks, the little girl saw some imitation pearl earrings in one of the store windows for $2. At that time, $2 was a lot of money, so her mom told her that they couldn't afford it at that moment but reminded her of her grandma's yearly Christmas gift of $1. She told her daughter that if she did a few chores, she would give her the other dollar she needed.

The little girl gets so excited and immediately sets out to do as many chores as she could and eventually collects a $1 bill from her grandma and her mother. As anticipated, the little girl buys the pearls, and she wears them everywhere; she literally wore them every where she went. She wore them to school, to church, to bed, in the bathtub...she loved them so much that she would never take them off.

One day her dad comes to her and asks her if he can have the pearls. This devastated the little girl because, even though she loved her father, she had worked hard to get her pearls and had no desire to let them go. So she tried to bargain with him and offered to give him her new baby doll with the pink pony instead. Her father declined.

About a month later, her dad came back again and asked his daughter, "Do you love me?"

"Yes, Dad, I love you," she said.

"Do you really love me?" he asked.

"Yes, Dad. I really love you," she told him.

"Ok. Do this for me. Let me have those two pearl earrings," he said.

"Daddy, I love you, but...I can't give you these pearl earrings, Daddy. I worked hard for them and Grandma gave me the extra dollar," she said.

The dad said, "Ok," and kissed her goodnight.

Two weeks later, her dad came home, and she was sitting in the living room shaking and crying. Her dad asked, "Baby, what's wrong?" She said, "Daddy, you remember when you asked me for the pearls?" "Yes, I remember," he answered.

The little girl stood up, reached for her daddy's hand and said, "Daddy, I love you." The little girl placed the pearls in her daddy's hand.

And while she was giving her father the pearls, he began to smile and he took the pearls with his left hand, but with his right hand he pulled out a velvet box. He handed the box to his daughter and told her to open it.

The little girl opened the box and a tear began to fall down her cheek. The father, showing his daughter the two fake pearl earrings in his left hand, asked, "Do you remember when I first asked you for these?"

The little girl nodded, "Yes."

"Well, I had these waiting for you the whole time," the father said as he reached into the velvet box and pulled out a genuine pearl necklace and placed it around his daughter's neck. "But because you weren't willing to give me those, I couldn't give you the real thing."

The moral of the story is that she wasn't willing to give up what she had not knowing that if she had given those things up that she had something better coming. Some of you will never be able to get on that next level, because there are some things that you're just not willing to let go of (i.e., your time, your energy, your talent, your money) because you feel like you've earned it, or you've forgotten where you came from, or are too consumed with stabilizing your financial status. At any given moment anyone else could be in your shoes, doing your job, building your home, loving your friends. But somehow, they chose you. Your boss chose you; your mate chose you; your friends chose you. Never forget that it wasn't you, but mercy and grace that is responsible for you being where you are.

> Greatness is understanding the importance of service and selfless acts as being necessary for the betterment of all mankind.

Spend time today reflecting on your actions this week.

Did you meet the challenge? If not, why?

SUMMARY OF THE WEEK

ENTITLED MINDSET vs GRATITUDE MINDSET

IDENTIFY

5 AREAS IN YOUR LIFE WHERE YOU FUNCTION AS THOUGH YOU ARE **OWED SOMETHING**

5 AREAS IN YOUR LIFE WHERE YOU FUNCTION AS THOUGH YOU ARE **GRATEFUL AND EAGER TO SERVE**

> Do you live mostly with an attitude that says you are owed something or is your life a life filled with expressions of gratitude and service?

GOT TO DO   GET TO DO

WHAT SIDE OF THE SPECTRUM CONSUMES MORE OF YOUR LIFE?

GREATNESS IS UPON YOU
CERTIFICATE OF COMPLETION

This is to certify that

_____

has successfully completed this week's challenge.

Eric Thomas and Associates, LLC

_____
signature

_____
date

WEEK 11

WORDS OF GREATNESS

LURK

to lie or wait in concealment; remain in or around a place

LURKER VS. HUNTER

Round 1

Are you waiting for your next meal or are you going out to catch it?

There are some chances in life that we take when we make the decision to move or to wait on certain opportunities. Both decisions have their risks, but this week we look at the dangers of waiting for certain opportunities and the danger of becoming complacent with the ones we've already been given.

*The next three chapter are intended to be learned as a unit, for this reason the activities are not sectioned according to days but the development process is the same.

WEEK 11

"If you don't hunt it down and kill it, it will hunt you down and kill you."

Flannery O'Connor

SURVIVE THE FITTEST - THE SWAMP

"I hate Mondays." This was the comment that turned the heads of two of my employees one day while walking up the steps of a barbershop on their lunch break. Saying "I hate Mondays" in front of any member of my team is like an Apple employee walking into an Apple store with a Samsung phone...it just doesn't happen. But on this day, it did. My Media Director, Karl, didn't know what to do with himself. He wasn't necessarily shocked to hear that someone hated Mondays, many people do, but he saw this as an opportunity to hopefully bring a different perspective to someone who was in need. And what better day is there to plant a seed of hope than a Monday?

"Why don't you like Mondays?" Karl asked, stopping on the stoop.

"Because you're starting the same damn thing all over again," the guy answered as he flicked his cigar out into the street and walked inside the shop.

"It's all about your perspective." Karl said, following him in. "But you have to see Mondays for what they are. It's your one chance to start the week out strong. It signifies new beginnings...new opportunities. Whatever you weren't able to perfect last week, today is the day to grind and get it right!"

He wasn't in the shop long before Karl realized that this young man had a three-year-old daughter who he hadn't seen since the day she was born.

"Wow," the barber said, clearing a space for him in his chair. "Why haven't you seen her? Is her mom keeping you away from her?"

"No, she lives all the way out west," he said.

"Really? West Coast? California?" Karl asked.

"What? No, west side about 20 miles from here," he answered.

"Wait...your daughter lives 20 miles from here, and you haven't seen her since she was born?" Karl asked in shock more so than judgment.

"With the paychecks I bring home, I can barely afford this haircut," he said leaning back in the chair. I don't have the gas money to be going back and forth, and I don't have a regular job; if I had a job, I'd go out there," he said.

"Ay man, if you need a job, I've got a few things you can do around the shop to make some extra cash," the barber offered.

"I appreciate it, but no thanks. It's not what I'm looking for right now. I mean, if someone gave me $50K tomorrow, I would take it. But until then...I'm cool. I can't afford to be making minimum wage," he said.

This guy was unsatisfied with the job he had, wanted more money, but was waiting on the "right" opportunity.

As I listened to Karl vent about his frustrations with the guy at the barbershop, my thoughts couldn't help but to land on a sign that I saw on the way to the airport in Florida a few days back: Crocodile SEEN IN THIS AREA: BE SAFE! Aside from the sense of relief that I felt knowing that I was being as compliant as possible as we drove 80mph past the warning sign, it made me think of that scene from the Disney movie, *Peter Pan,* where the Crocodile would be lurking in the water waiting for an opportunity to attack Hook.

> I had to learn that I wasn't getting as far as I wanted to go because I was complacent

While the young man in the barbershop upset Karl, I actually understood where he was coming from. Personal issues aside, he had a mindset that many people have. Of course, it's manifested in different ways, but the truth is that most people hate Mondays, and if given the opportunity for instant gratification, they'd take it. Right or wrong, it's not uncommon. The question is, are you courageous enough to look at your life and identify the Crocodile in you?

LEARN IT

Early in my career, I had to learn that I wasn't getting as far as I wanted to go because I was complacent - I had characteristics of the lurking Crocodile:

Crocodiles can sit and wait for days for an opportunity to eat.

I was always in waiting mode - I waited for the phone to ring; I waited for someone to mentor me into Greatness; I waited on the approval of others; and I waited for directives.

And once they finally eat, they can go weeks without eating again.

When I first started my career, my speaking engagements would be weeks, sometimes months apart from each other. And at the time, I wasn't doing anything to change that. I was simply content with the engagements I received.

Crocodiles aren't able to attack unless their prey is in their immediate area.

Even when I did begin to crave new opportunities, I didn't go out of my way to seek them out. I only jumped on top of those things that I knew were readily available to me (i.e., conferences that I knew were coming to town, schools that were in my immediate area, etc.).

Crocodiles have to wait for the right moment to "strike", otherwise, their prey may get away.

I was very slow when it came to getting on board of new speaking opportunities that were unfamiliar to me. My fear was that if I did the unfamiliar and messed up that no other opportunities would come.

In short, when I first began my speaking career, I had a Lurker's mentality. I waited for the opportunities I dreamed of having. This mindset almost destroyed my career. We've all been there at some point in life. But before we can change it, we must first acknowledge those areas in our life where the Lurker's mentality exist.

In the space provided below, address what area in your life the Lurker's mindset is active in. Then address how this mentality has hindered your growth. Additional space is provided in your GIUY Success Journal.

I probably have a "Lurker's" mentality because ...

_____

_____

_____

How has this mentality hindered my growth?

_____

_____

_____

ACCEPT IT

It was hard, but I had to accept that there was a time in my life when I behaved like the Crocodile. For me, it wasn't that waiting for an opportunity to speak at certain types of events was a bad thing, but I couldn't help but to think about all the opportunities I was missing out on by not seeking out what I wanted.

What opportunities are you waiting on? What opportunities have you taken advantage of and then became satisfied? Why is that?

I accept that I am presently waiting on the following

opportunities :

_____

_____

I accept that I took advantage of the following

opportunities and became satisfied once I achieved:

_____

_____

Identify areas in your life where you have failed to take initiative and, as a result, missed a golden opportunity.

How has that hindered the growth of your company or the people you work with?

EMBRACE IT

Waiting takes time. We miss out on so many opportunities simply because they're not within our immediate reach.

Lurkers perceive time as though it lasts forever. Like the circular clock above, time is never ending for them.

When you move from the perspective of the hour glass, every second counts - you don't have time to spare.

Which time piece do you operate from? What concrete examples can you pull from to support your answer?

CHANGE IT

Using the information you wrote about in the "Embrace It" exercise, write about how you can aggressively seek out each opportunity you're lurking for. Pair each moment you're waiting on with the appropriate aggressive attack.

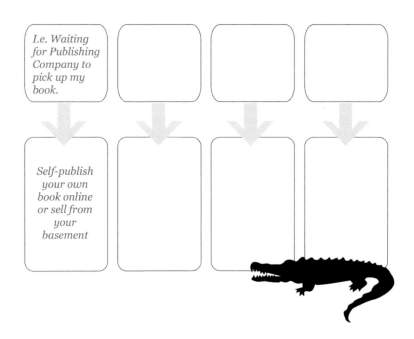

LIVE IT

Create a 7-day plan to get rid of your Lurker's Mentality.

SUNDAY   *i.e., Write my 7-day plan ...*
_____

_____

*Use your GIUY Success Journal to write out your plan.

GREATNESS IS...

There was a King who was unlike any other king the people had heard of because He didn't live in a castle, He didn't wear the fancy clothes, and He didn't use his power in the traditional sense. But what He had, which piqued the curiosity of the people in his city, was the ability to change lives. So he walked the streets of city after city, teaching and healing those He would encounter and as word got around of His presence and the incredible things He was doing for the people, multitudes began to follow Him because they wanted to know and understand more and they wanted to be healed.

The King, seeing the crowd, decided to walk up a mountain. As He journeyed, the multitudes of people who were just moments earlier, following the King, asking and begging for more information and more healing, remained behind and watched Him as He made his move up the mount. The King sat on the mountain knowing that only those who really wanted the wisdom He was getting ready to share would be willing and courageous enough to follow Him; the others would remain behind and wait for those who received the wisdom to bring the information back down the mountain. Some of them would do this because they were afraid to make the sacrifice of climbing the mountain, some of them stayed behind because they were content with just being in the atmosphere, some of them were too needy and insecure to take the hike, some of them weren't there to get information at all but just wanted to be seen with the crowd, and others of them knew that if they waited long enough, someone else would go and get what was needed and bring it down to the rest of them. When the King took His seat, only twelve of His followers came to Him - the King never called for them or tried to get their attention, they just came. And the King taught them as people of authority and not as mere scribes.

Which group would you have been a part of? Would you have been one of the twelve or a part of the remaining multitude?

Greatness is moving outside of your comfort zone, because out of your comfort zone is where the miracles happen. If it doesn't challenge you, it won't change you.

Spend time today reflecting on your actions this week.

Did you meet the challenge? If not, why?

_____

_____

_____

_____

_____

_____

_____

_____

_____

_____

_____

_____

SUMMARY OF THE WEEK

THE LURKING CROCODILE

Crocodiles can sit and wait for days for an opportunity to eat ...

WHAT ARE YOU WAITING FOR?

... and once they finally eat, they can go weeks without eating again...

Identify areas in your life where you have **failed to take initiative** and as a result

MISSED A GOLDEN OPPORTUNITY

Crocodiles aren't able to attack unless their prey is in their immediate area

IDENTIFY THOSE THINGS THAT YOU ARE GUILTY OF "LURKING" AROUND FOR

Crocodiles have to wait for the right moment to "strike", otherwise, their prey may get away.

HOW CAN YOU AGGRESSIVELY SEEK OUT EACH OPPORTUNITY YOU'RE LURKING FOR?

GREATNESS IS UPON YOU
CERTIFICATE OF COMPLETION

This is to certify that

_____

has successfully completed this week's challenge.

Eric Thomas and Associates, LLC

_____
signature

_____
date

WEEK

12

WORDS OF GREATNESS

HUNT
to chase or search for; seek; endeavor to obtain or find

LURKER VS. HUNTER

Round 2

Does your behavior say "I'm driven" or "I'm content"?

What really drives you and gets you moving? Remember, Lurkers sit and wait, but if you're really going to get ahead, there are some opportunities you're going to have to get up and take.

WEEK 12

"Passion and drive are not the same at all. Passion pulls you toward something you cannot resist. Drive pushes you toward something you feel compelled or obligated to do. If you know nothing about yourself, you can't tell the difference."

Randy Komisar

SURVIVE THE FITTEST - MISTISSINI ...

Quebec. I am fascinated by how quickly environments shift at the onset of an appetite. Indeed, the hungrier you are, the more endangered the object of your appetite becomes. This is a fundamental truth that exists equally among animals and man. In fact, Nature demands that we are strategic in conquering our conquest to ensure that we are in the best position to survive.

I had the honor one year of speaking at an event in Mistissini, Quebec. The gentlemen who made the arrangements picked me up from the airport to drive me out to their community. As we traveled, I noticed that there weren't very many restaurants along the way. This was disappointing to my subtlely growling stomach. Concerned about being impolite, I tried to camouflage my hunger by shifting positions in my seat and actively engaging in the ongoing conversation. But I realized my efforts were in vain when the guy sitting next to me looked at me and said, "Yeah, fast food spots are slim out this way, we mostly live off the land; but we prepared a huge dinner for you at the Banquet Hall. Everyone is really excited about tonight..." As he was talking, I found myself looking out of the window at miles and miles of beautiful green trees, clear blue bodies of water surrounded by pure white snowy mountains, to the backdrop of what would have to be one of the clearest blue skies I've ever seen...we were far from Detroit. "Living off the land" is not an expression that I recall ever being used by me and my friends when I was growing up in Detroit; and if it was, it had a completely different meaning. Here in Mistissini, people literally use the land for their needs - they fish, they hunt, and they gather - no factories, no super giant retail conglomerates - just the land.

"I can't wait to get there! It sounds like it's going to be a phenomenal night," I said, reuniting myself to the conversation.

Curious about experiencing food straight from the land, I asked, "What are we having tonight?"

"Oh, you're going to enjoy this! We're having fish chowder, geese, and Bear," he answered.

"Bear?" I asked.

Bear? I began thinking, if they live off the land and they're eating Bear, then that means that the Bear and the people are in the same community. Bears don't walk the streets of Detroit. As a matter of fact, outside of a few visits to the zoo and maybe a few episodes of *National Geographic*, I'd never seen a Bear before, so the idea of potentially encountering one left me a little unnerved.

Once again, as though he could read my thoughts, he said, "Don't be afraid."

"What?" I asked, taken off guard.

"There's nothing to be afraid of. This is hibernating season, so the odds of seeing one are really slim. If this were Spring, we wouldn't bring you out here because the odds of seeing one would be greater...they're more visible when they're hungry because they're always out looking for food," he said jokingly.

And with that statement, it was clear:

When a Bear is ready to be fed, he comes out of hibernation and, almost immediately, the environment changes. Strategies have to be used to compete for the same resources; different precautions are exercised by animals and man; gaming opportunities open up; and a sense of fear increases in some while excitement increases in others. All of these shifts occur for one reason: the Bear is hungry. And everything in that community understands what this means - adjust or deal with the consequences.

I admire the people of Mistissini. When I was homeless, I ate out of trashcans and encountered many ferocious people; and while I have been blessed to see many things, many of which I would gladly replace my homeless experience within a heartbeat, coming eye to eye with a hungry Bear is not one of those experiences.

LEARN IT

I remember three things from my Biology class in high school:

- Communities contain interacting populations of several different species.
- Populations cannot grow indefinitely, because the environment they live in contains a limited amount of food, water, living space, and other resources.
- When more than one population tries to use the same limited resources (i.e., food, water, etc.) it's called competition.

The biggest challenge that Lurkers have that a successful Hunter wouldn't is that Lurkers are at the mercy of whatever the competition has left behind. So while a Lurker may be waiting on someone to give him information about the next job opportunity, the Hunter has already sought them out and taken the ones he or she wants. Wile the Lurker is waiting for the "right time" to go back to school, start a new career, or work on his relationship with family or coworkers, the Hunter has already filled out and submitted the applications, went on the job interview, and planned a family gathering or corporate luncheon.

Opportunities are limited so if you're going to make it to that next level, you're going to need the drive of a Hunter. Like the Bear, whole environments should shift once you make a move.

When it comes to your career, school, or your personal life, who do you identify more with, the Lurker (Crocodile) or the Hunter (Bear)?

CHARACTERISTICS OF LURKERS AND HUNTERS

LURKER	HUNTER
Wait for opportunities to come to them.	*Looks for opportunities or creates his or her own.*
Becomes complacent after seizing an opportunity.	*Is never satisfied.*
Waits for the right moment to "strike" from fear of a missed opportunity.	*Takes Action: "All In" or nothing at all*

Who do you have in your life who would stand to benefit from your having a Hunter's Mentality?

_____

_____

_____

What have you lost by allowing yourself to behave like a Lurker? You may use your answer(s) from last week.

_____

_____

ACCEPT AND EMBRACE IT

Your will to thrive and survive must be greater than any obstacle you face. The thing you live for must mean more to you than the thing that seeks to destroy you. What's been more dominant in your life, your fears and failures or your "Why"? What drives you?

_____

_____

_____

The key to developing a Hunter's Mentality is to push yourself from within. There are eight factors that will help to intensify your drive and get you moving like a Hunter:

Self regulation

Otherwise known as "self-control." Hunters have to be disciplined to survive.

Self motivation

If you have to wait on others to motivate you, then you're displaying characteristics of a Lurker. The better you are at motivating yourself, the quicker you'll be able to go out and grab your opportunities.

Self governance

You create the rules. You set the tone. Because of the nature of Lurkers, their "next big break" is decided for them - their whole day is centered around whether or not an opportunity is presented to them. Hunters make decisive decisions about what direction they're going in and don't have to wait to be instructed.

Focus

Hunters have the ability to set their goals and keep their eyes on them.

Personal excellence

Personal excellence isn't about perfection. It's about perfecting everything that you set out to do. If you've committed to it in some way, you put forth your total effort in making sure that it represents who you are.

Personal best

You are your biggest competition. Hunters are never satisfied, because they know that they are only as good as their last conquest.

Failures

Just because you've failed, it doesn't make you a failure. Resilience is an integral part of the hunt. The tragedy is not in falling, it's in falling and refusing to get up.

The success of others

Seeing other people succeed should make you even more hungry for the hunt. Set their success as the bar and then pass it. Don't forget to reach back and give them a hand when you do.

In the speedometers below, indicate where you stand in terms of your drive in each of the areas listed. Don't just rate yourself in these areas. Take time to consider why you scored yourself the way that you did. For instance, if you give yourself an 8 in terms of your drive to be focused on your goals, then think about the reasons why you aren't a 10. Have you always been an 8?

The tragedy is not in falling, it's in falling and refusing to get up.

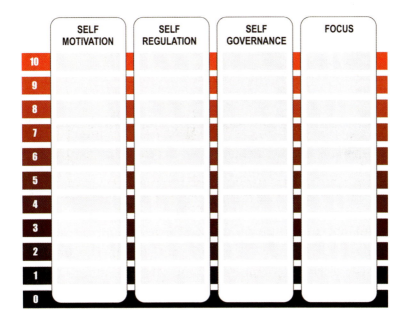

_____

_____

_____

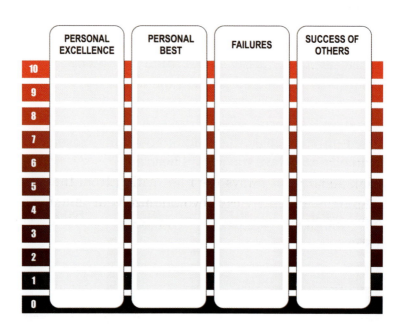

_____

_____

_____

CHANGE IT

List the top 10 most destructive habits that are suffocating your drive and hindering your Hunter's Mindset. What's keeping you from getting to where you need to be at this point in your life? Use your Success Journal for your answers.

1. _____
2. _____
3. _____
4. _____
5. _____
6. _____
7. _____

Think about 3 to 5 ways the information from the Accept It/Embrace It activity can revolutionize your thinking and shift your behavior. Use your Success Journal for your answers.

1. _____
2. _____

LIVE IT

Now that you know what intensifies your drive and the obstacles that hinder your drive and, in turn, your ability to hunt, create a 7-day plan to help you stay on track to having a Hunter's Mentality.

SUNDAY   *i.e., Write my 7-day plan ...* _____

_____

*Use your GIUY Success Journal to write out your plan.

GREATNESS IS...

"Do something."

These two words, in my opinion, are the most powerful words in the movie, John Q. I've watched a few movies in my day and none have moved me in the way that John Q has. Every time I think about taking a day off or not being productive in some fashion, I remember that scene where Denzel's wife looks at him after finding out that their son only has hours to live, and she says those two words.

In two words, she conveyed what it means to be a Hunter: take action. And because of this, her husband, who at one point was waiting for things to happen, experiences a shift in mentality and seeks out a means to get things done. I am not saying that his actions should be duplicated, but I am saying that the mind shift from Lurker to Hunter was captivating, because it sends the message that even if you are a Lurker in most aspects of your life, when given the proper motivation, you have the power to go out and hunt.

What if your son, daughter, or someone really significant in your life needed something that was life changing and all that was required of you was to focus in a way that you have never focused before... no snooze button and no extra day off? What if their well- being or your ability to increase the quality of your own life was predicated on your performance? What shift is going to have to happen in your life for you to take action? What needs to happen to get you to stop hitting the snooze button?

Greatness is deciding to take action, not just for your life, but for the lives of those who depend on you.

Spend time today reflecting on your actions this week.

Did you meet the challenge? If not, why?

_____

_____

SUMMARY OF THE WEEK

Lurkers are at the mercy of whatever the competition has left behind. Who do you identify with?

THE LURKER (Crocodile)   or   **THE HUNTER (Bear)**

FEARS & FAILURE

YOUR WHY

The thing you live for must mean more to you than the thing that seeks to destroy you.

WHAT'S BEEN MORE DOMINANT IN YOUR LIFE?

- self motivate
- focuses outside of money that drives you
- personal excellence

BEAR MINDED

- self regulate
- self governed
- personal best
- failure
- others success

PUSH YOURSELF FROM WITHIN

GREATNESS IS UPON YOU
CERTIFICATE OF COMPLETION

This is to certify that

_____

has successfully completed this week's challenge.

Eric Thomas and Associates, LLC

_____
signature

_____
date

WEEK 13

WORDS OF GREATNESS

JUNGLE
something made up of many confused elements; a bewildering complex or maze

LURKER VS. HUNTER

Round 3

How do you get along with the opposing forces of the Jungle?

You may realize that you're a Lurker but need some time to transition from that mindset; in the meantime, how do you function in an office with a Bear? Or perhaps you mostly function as a Hunter but find yourself frustrated by the complacency of the Crocodiles in your environment and need to understand how to cope better. This week we take a deeper look at the different type of relationships that can exist between the Crocodile and the Bear in the office.

WEEK 13

"Coming together is a beginning; keeping together is progress; working together is success."

Henry Ford

SURVIVAL OF THE FITTEST - THE JUNGLE EXPERIENCE

In the office, when the Bear and the Crocodile are forced to work together tension can only be expected, because their feeding styles are so vastly different, and yet everyone must eat. As a Lurker, the Crocodile waits in anticipation for his meal and can be satisfied for days before he feels the need to eat again. They don't seek out new opportunities for the company or bring fresh ideas to the table. This is frustrating for the Hunter, who spends most of his time traveling long distances in search of food (i.e., new clients, new opportunities, new ideas to increase productivity and efficiency).

While this duality can be seen across the board in many relationships and professional environments, this is the primary basis for the disconnect between CEO's and their employees in terms of how they operate within the company. The CEO, in his habitat, is constantly on the move, seeking out new opportunities to bring revenue to the company.

Unfortunately, the challenge that many CEOs have with their employees is that while they are out, constantly hunting and searching for partnerships, investment opportunities, and forging relationships that will benefit the company, many of their employees are back in the office lurking - waiting for the next opportunity to come to them. This frustrates the CEO as he is constantly faced with the pressure to hunt - and hunt well because the life of his company depends on it; and he does so with the knowledge that, at best, only a handful of his employees are also huntsmen, the other 75-80% are composed of either employees who are capable of hunting but don't know how or employees who are plain and simply comfortable with being Lurkers.

The great controversy between CEO's and employees is that often times it seems that their value systems are misaligned:

- CEO's want employees to be able to work and forecast new opportunities at the same time.
- Employees need to designate a set time to do one or the other.
- CEO's want employees to constantly look for ways to be efficient and productive and look ahead.
- Employees, because of the time constraints and nature of their jobs, aren't able to look ahead as frequently or with as much precision as their employer would like.

Often it seems that employees want their boss to be under "covenant" while they remain under "contract" (View Week 19). Meaning, employees demand to be paid on time; they want bonuses, raises, promotions, etc. but don't have the same expectations as to their commitment (i.e., timeliness, meeting deadlines, increasing productivity).

Many employees come to work on Friday, but they don't finish the day as strong as they started the week. As a result, productivity is stilted, time is lost, and the ever burdensome hamster wheel spins relentlessly on its axle forcing CEOs to make "life or death" decisions to preserve the company and, in truth, their sanity. I call this phenomenon The Jungle Experience.

LEARN IT

> Productivity is optimized when everyone understands how their role affects the organization.

The Jungle Experience does not have to be as chaotic as it seems. Productivity is optimized when everyone understands how their behavior affects the organization. Looking at the employee in relation to the company as a whole, this can be illustrated through the concept of symbiotic relationships. A symbiotic relationship is a close association between two or more different organisms; the relationships are either one of mutualism, commensalism, or parasitism. A similar concept can be applied to employees and the companies they work for.

Parasitic

Parasitic relationships are those relationships where one organism benefits and the other organism is harmed. In the office, parasites are those people who directly benefit from the company while simultaneously harming the company in the process. Parasites impede productivity by coming to work late, they only half do their job, making it necessary for others to double up on work in order to keep productivity at a competitive rate, they're generally uncooperative with colleagues, and have issues with authority; these behaviors cost the company money as hours are spent trying to placate the parasite or remedy some issue caused by his or her inability to cooperate or take instruction. Time is wasted thus productivity decreases. They are the ultimate Lurkers.

Commensalism

In commensalism, one organism benefits and the other organism isn't harmed, but it also doesn't benefit. Here, the employee neither harms nor benefits the company. Several companies fall victim to this relationship especially, because no noticeable harm is being done to the company (at least not right away). Many Crocodiles fall into this category. For example, I worked with a company when we first launched Eric Thomas and Associates, LLC, that was responsible for doing PR work on our behalf. I found that instead of going out and finding new promotional opportunities, the PR company only moved on the opportunities that came to me from other sources. This didn't hurt the company, because CJ and LaShanna continued to work to push the brand, but it didn't help us either. The extra work that my team put in could've been used for other projects and services. I was still paying the company for its services because they were at a minimum, contacting radio and TV stations who had already contacted me, but my company was in no better position because of the PR company. Employees in this category aren't harmful to the company, but they simply aren't helpful either. This is where you will find most of your complacent Lurkers. But beware, this is dangerous because

Productivity is at its highest when benefits are mutually exchanged.

of the missed opportunities that go undiscovered. For this reason, it can be just as crucial as a parasitic relationship.

Mutualism

In a mutual relationship, both parties involved benefit from the other. Productivity is at its highest when benefits are mutually exchanged. Employees not only execute on assignments/projects, they actively seek out other avenues to bring innovative and creative ideas to the table. They come to work early and leave late, they are initiators by nature and are self motivated. In this relationship, time is well spent, and productivity and profits increase. In exchange, employers are in a position to increase benefits and salaries. Bear-minded people (Hunters) dominate this category.

ACCEPT IT

Think about your performance in relationship to your company or organization. Which symbiotic relationship best describes how you function with your team?

- PARASITISM
- COMMENSALISM
- MUTUALISM

What are you doing in your work environment to cause you to relate to that group? Be specific.

_____

_____

EMBRACE IT

Find someone at your job or organization who is better than you at functioning in a mutually beneficial capacity and ask him or her what obstacles he or she had to overcome in order to get to their position. Was his or her relationship with the company always mutual? How did the person move from being parasitic or having a commensalism relationship with the company?

_____

_____

_____

CHANGE IT

Recite the following:

"I know that I am able to have a mutually beneficial relationship within my company or organization. I can do the following things to accomplish this goal (i.e., come to work, take an appropriate length lunch break, etc.)":

_____

_____

_____

Identify your behaviors that contribute to a more parasitic relationship.

_____

_____

_____

LIVE IT

Remember, mutual relationships benefit both parties involved. Profits and productivity are maximized when employees feel that they are getting the most out of their careers (i.e., salaries, benefits, growth opportunities, etc.) and CEOs feel that they are getting the most out of their investment in the employees' skills, talents, and potential. Create a 7-day plan that you will use to help you to move toward a stronger mutual relationship between you and your company or organization.

SUNDAY *i.e., Write my 7-day plan ...*
_____

_____

*Use your GIUY Success Journal to write out your plan.

GREATNESS IS...

There's a story of a man who was once the Judge over a whole nation and, because of his physical strength, was able to single handedly defeat his nation's enemies one by one. The mystery behind his strength was one of grave concern to the enemy camp. They knew that if they could find his weakness, they would be able to overtake him, and such would end his reign over his Nation.

When the enemies learned of the Judge's affair with a woman in a neighboring village, they saw this as an opportunity to get the information they needed to bring about the Judge's demise. They offered the woman a large sum of money to join their scheme to uncover the secret to the Judge's great strength.

Weak in his affection towards the woman, the Judge eventually gave in to her persistent requests to know what made him so powerful. He confessed that the secret to his strength was in his hair - he took a vow at birth that his hair would never be touched.

Later that night, while asleep, the woman called out for her coconspirators. She told them the Judge's secret, and they shaved off his hair and bound him. Now weak and defenseless, the Judge was captured and the Nation that he had spent his life trying to protect, was left vulnerable to the attacks of their enemy.

Listen, things didn't fall apart for the Judge because he fell in love, and it didn't fall apart simply because he allowed himself to trust someone. The issue developed when he attached himself to a relationship that was one sided. When we aren't aware of the nature of our relationships, we put ourselves in the position to not only be deceived but to be destroyed. He allowed himself to connect with someone who cared more about what she could get out of him than what she could give him. She didn't care about his goals and dreams or even his safety. She was the ultimate parasite.

Our feelings, our desire to make money, our desire to avoid hurting others' feelings, our need to get out of uncomfortable situations, etc. can function to not only blind us to the true nature of people, they are also the reasons why we sometimes latch on to relationships (personal and professional) in a way that can be detrimental. You don't want to be the parasite any more than you want to be the victim of the parasite.

Greatness is valuing the rewards of a mutual relationship over selfish ambition.

Spend time today reflecting on your actions this week.

Did you meet the challenge? If not, why?

_____

_____

_____

_____

_____

_____

_____

_____

_____

_____

SUMMARY OF THE WEEK

SYMBIOTIC RELATIONSHIPS

Which best describes how you function with your team?

PARASITISM
one organism benefits and the other organism is harmed

Identify your behaviors that contribute to a more parasitic relationship

COMMENSALISM
one organism benefits and the other organism isn't harmed but it also doesn't benefit from it

Find someone who is better than you at functioning in a mutually beneficial capacity

MUTUALISM
both parties involved benefit from the other

Create a 21-day plan that you will use to help you to move toward a stronger mutual relationship

GREATNESS IS UPON YOU
CERTIFICATE OF COMPLETION

This is to certify that

_____

has successfully completed this week's challenge.

Eric Thomas and Associates, LLC

_____
signature

_____
date

WEEK

14

WORDS OF GREATNESS

GURU
an intellectual guide or leader

SINK VS. SWIM

Do you behave as though you've already learned all that you need to learn or are you open to new information?

No one knows everything and if you think you do, you're cheating yourself. For some of us, the key to success isn't about seizing opportunities or overcoming complacency. For some, success will come as soon as you realize that you're not as together as you think you are and you're brave enough to seek out help.

WEEK 14

"If there is no struggle, there is no progress."

Frederick Douglas

LEARN TO BREATHE

Who Wants to Be a Millionaire was possibly one of the best game shows of its time for one simple reason: it gave people the opportunity to use their intellect to become millionaires while acknowledging the likelihood that they may not be able to do it on their own. The contestant may have been the smartest person in their class or held the record in random trivia, but almost always, at some point in the game, they had to use a Lifeline.

Contrary to what many believe, there is always someone smarter, faster, more educated, or more talented than you. But this revelation is not a moment of shame - it's actually the opposite. People mistakenly believe that success is tied up in their own intelligence and abilities, but the truth is that success is obtained in one's ability to grow. And growth means constantly seeking out new information and guidance on how to improve. This is possibly the most difficult chapter in this book, because it requires you to understand that you're not as great as you think you are and the only way to become greater, is to accept it. To do this, there are some character flaws that you have to be willing to face and let go of (i.e., pride), but when you do... WHEW... Success awaits you!

DAY ONE: LEARN IT

Having a mentor is a great step in facilitating your personal and professional development. The concept of having a Mentor goes all the way back to Plato and Socrates. Mentors are a great resource to new information and potentially golden gateways to success, because if you pay attention to them, you not only gain a wealth of information, but you also get to learn from their mistakes.

Researching

Researching new ways to test and stretch your abilities is also a great way to build on what you already know. I spend hours reading newspaper articles, books, and magazines of different genres. I try to never assume anything, and I look for ways to challenge myself and my team with new and innovative information.

Asking questions

Asking questions of the people who are already where you want to be is priceless. Every time I meet someone who has accomplished something different from me, I ask, "How did you do it?" "What road did you take?" "What were the challenges?" "How did you overcome them?" Sometimes the information isn't for me. There have been several times when I've asked these questions of people who are doing things that other people in my life aspire to do, and so I ask them so that I can bring the information back to my loved ones and help them to grow. The growth of the people in my environment is equally important to me, because no one wants to be a giant in a field of dwarfs... it's counterproductive.

What steps are you taking to stretch yourself?

DAY TWO: ACCEPT IT

Repeat this phrase out loud three times: *I'm good at what I do, but I don't know everything.*

Now, fill in the blanks below.
I am very skilled at

_____

_____

and

_____

Even so, I accept the fact that I don't know all there is to know about these areas, and I understand that there are others who know more and who may be better at them than me.

Before you can begin to move in the direction of growth, there may be some things that you have to let go of to get started. For example, pride, arrogance, or an inflated ego are popular obstacles that get in the way of a person being able to seek out other sources for help.

Accepting this does not make me less of a person nor does it lessen my abilities.

I will let go of the following things

_____

_____

and

_____

to help myself grow in these areas.

DAY THREE: EMBRACE IT

Now that you've accepted that you don't know everything, and you've identified the obstacles in your life that keep you from seeking out opportunities to grow in your field, find someone who you can talk to who is considered to be an expert in the area you're interested in (i.e., CEO of a company, an acclaimed author, professor, or someone whose marital or parental life you admire). Speak to the person and ask the questions you've been dying to know the answers to.

DAY FOUR: CHANGE IT

Even experts consult other experts in their field to bounce ideas off of and to learn new information. When you're trying to get to another level of success, the question isn't always, "What am I doing wrong?"; sometimes it's about "What am I doing right?" or "What am I doing that other people are also doing?" or "Who's doing more and why is it working for them?"

Today, we're going to deal with the positive, but before we journey there, take a look at the diagram below. Assess where you fall on the Guru-Meter.

- A Novice is still getting to know his craft; he may perform well in it but still has a lot to learn.
- A Master knows his craft very well, but he is not able to teach it to others for the purpose of duplication.
- An Expert not only knows his craft, but he can teach it to others so well that they can duplicate the process.

Now, take a moment to write about the positive things you're working on to get you on the path to Greatness. Where did you fall on the Guru-Meter concerning those things? What sources do you need to get or who do you need to talk to so you can get to the next level?

_____

_____

_____

_____

_____

DAY FIVE: LIVE IT

Admitting that you don't know it all is only the first step. Now, create a 7-day plan using the information from Day One to help you climb the Guru-Ladder.

SUNDAY   *i.e., Write my 7-day plan ...*
_____

*Use your GIUY Success Journal to write out your plan.

GREATNESS IS...

In my autobiography, The Secret to Success, *I tell this story about a Guru and a young man who wanted to be successful. The young man seeks out the Guru to learn the mystery behind his success. Eager for the opportunity to get ahead, he meets the Guru at the beach, anxiously anticipating his lesson. The Guru, older, wiser, and unrestrained, looks the young man straight in his eyes and asks, "How bad do you want to be successful?" Giving it little to no thought, the young man answers, "Real bad." To his surprise, the Guru takes him by the hand and leads him out into the deep parts of the water.*

When they were a little more than waist deep, the Guru grabs the young man, takes his head, and holds it down under the water. The young man, beating and slapping the water, fights to resist the Guru's attack; but he finds no relief until the Guru lets him up and asks him, "What was the one thing you wanted while you were under water?"

Gasping and wheezing for air, his heart racing partly from his struggle under water and partly from the uncertainty of what the Guru would do to him next, the young man stammers, "I wanted to breathe." Pleased, the Guru responded, "When you want to succeed as bad as you want to breathe, then you'll be successful."

Consider the things you have done to work towards your goals (i.e., classes you've taken, study time, overtime, investment of money, etc.). While his approach, to some, may seem unorthodox, the Guru was making a phenomenal point: we say we want success, we say we want to move to the next level... to step our game up, but most of us aren't willing to do what it will take to get there.

The biggest deterrent for many of us is our pride. We think we know more, we think we can do more, we think we're smarter, and more talented than the next guy. The thing that changed the young man's life wasn't just in the lesson he was taught, it was in the fact that he sought out the Guru to begin with. He needed to know something, and he was smart enough to know that he didn't have the answer, and so he searched for the person who did.

Greatness is acknowledging that as talented and successful as you may be, there is someone else who can show you more.

Spend time today reflecting on your actions this week.

Did you meet the challenge? If not, why?

SUMMARY OF THE WEEK

HAVING A MENTOR
a great step in facilitating your personal and professional development.

RESEARCHING — Researching new ways to test and stretch your abilities is also a great way to build on what you already know.

ASKING — Asking questions of the people who are already where you want to be is priceless

Before you can begin to move in the direction of

gROWTH
there may be some things that you have to let go of to get started

GURU-METER
where do you fall?

NOVICE   MASTER   EXPERT

GREATNESS IS UPON YOU
CERTIFICATE OF COMPLETION

This is to certify that

_____

has successfully completed this week's challenge.

Eric Thomas and Associates, LLC

_____
signature

_____
date

WEEK 15

WORDS OF GREATNESS

ATTRACT

to draw by appealing to the emotions or senses, by stimulating interest, or by exciting admiration

REPEL VS. ATTRACT

Finding the right mentor can be a long and tedious process. What if they're too busy or live too far away? How can you take advantage of the Mentor's wisdom if you can never talk to them? In the previous chapter we talked about the importance of seeking out help; this week, we discuss what you can do to bring your guru to you.

WEEK 15

"People ask me all the time how they can find their Guru or mentor. The answer is simple. You attract what you are"

Eric Thomas

ATTRACTING YOUR GURU

Seeking out a mentor is a great way to cultivate your success story. But seeking a mentor can be a hard and arduous task. Your time spent may prove more effective if you're able to make sure that once you've made the decision to seek out help, still make your primary focus the pursuit of your passion...pursued in the spirit of Excellence.

I have a guru story of my own. CJ, who is now the President of Eric Thomas and Associates, LLC., was a student at Michigan State University while I was teaching and advising students there. Although I had not met CJ yet, I kept hearing about this young man who was making major power moves on Campus as it related to the development of African American males, an area that I was also working in and passionate about.

People would come up to me all the time and ask me, "Have you ever met CJ? He would be a great addition to the work you are doing." Being extremely busy at the time, having recently relocated my entire family to Michigan, I didn't have time to go hunt this young man down, but I was very interested in meeting him and seeing what all the fuss was about.

A few weeks went by, and I was speaking at a conference for African American males. Afterwards, a man came up to me and asked if I knew his son, CJ, who was a student at MSU and had won several awards for his mentoring work in the community. I responded that I had not, but that I had heard about him on several occasions. I then gave him my contact information and told him to have his son connect with me first thing Monday morning.

Sure enough, Monday morning rolled around and CJ walked in my office. Before I could greet him, he said, "Man, I've been hearing so much about you! It's good to finally meet you." I just laughed as if to say, "Ditto." He told me he was having little success finding a mentor on campus, and he would love to link up and share some ideas. The rest, as they say, is history!

CJ and I went on to build the largest retention program on campus with me as the advisor and him as my student liaison. After graduating, CJ became the president of Eric Thomas and Associates, LLC. and is not only my business partner, but also my protege and little brother.

DAY ONE: LEARN IT

I told you that the previous chapter was possibly the hardest chapter because you have to be honest with yourself and admit that you don't know everything. Once you do this, growth is easy. What I want you to get from my story about CJ is that CJ, like many of you, was seeking a mentor. The difference is, he wasn't waiting on a mentor, nor did he spend all of his time and energy looking for one.

He was following his own passion and operating in a spirit of excellence and, in turn, he attracted a mentor.

The question today is simple: What are you doing to attract your mentor? Are you inactively sitting and waiting for your guru to show up? Or are you living your dream and creating the opportunity that could change your life?

DAY TWO: ACCEPT IT

Even when you find a mentor, the time you have together is ineffective if you don't know what you're looking to learn. Today, think through the process. If you were to meet your mentor today (or if you were able to spend a whole day with your current mentor), what would you want to learn? What areas in your life would you want direction on? Create a Mentor Wish List. Remember, this list is not about the characteristics you want in a mentor. This list is about the information you hope to gain from having a mentor.

_____

_____

_____

DAY THREE: EMBRACE IT

Find out what makes the Greats in your field Great. Find out what schools they attended, what books they read, what hobbies they had, and model their behaviors.

DAY FOUR: CHANGE IT

Get out and volunteer your time in your field of interest. Show people that this is not just something you are looking to make some money doing but rather something that you are passionate and excited about. Make them ask the question, "Man, have you heard of _____?"

DAY FIVE: LIVE IT

What strategy can you create and implement to attract your guru to you?

SUNDAY   *i.e., Write my 7-day plan ...*

*Use your GIUY Success Journal to write out your plan.

GREATNESS IS...

"Phil Jackson. Phil Jackson is a – to me, he's a professional Dean Smith. He challenged me mentally, not just physically..."
[Excerpt from Michael Jordan's Basketball Hall of Fame Enshrinement Speech]

You've heard the story: Michael Jordan didn't make the Varsity team of his high school basketball team when he first started out. But he stayed in the game and continued to play anyway. He pursued his passion, gave 120% in every game and, in doing so, his efforts eventually made way for him to meet his mentor, Phil Jackson.

The rest is history.

Greatness is learning to seek the information while also acting on the body of knowledge you already have.

Spend time today reflecting on your actions this week.

Did you meet the challenge? If not, why?

_____

_____

_____

_____

_____

SUMMARY OF THE WEEK

WHAT ARE YOU DOING TO ATTRACT YOUR MENTOR

WHAT WOULD YOU WANT TO LEARN

CREATE A MENTOR WISH LIST

NETWORK in your field

Find out what makes THE GREATS IN YOUR FIELD GREAT

VOLUNTEER YOUR TIME

Show people that this is not just something you are looking to make some money doing but rather something that you are passionate and excited about.

GREATNESS IS UPON YOU
CERTIFICATE OF COMPLETION

This is to certify that

_____

has successfully completed this week's challenge.

Eric Thomas and Associates, LLC

_____
signature

_____
date

WEEK

16

WORDS OF GREATNESS

EXECUTE

To perform or carry out what is required

STAY VS. GO

Does the thought of a new beginning scare you or excite you?

The hardest, simplest thing in life is to leave everything behind and start something new. I know because I did it. And so can you. In this chapter, we are going to discuss how to effectively begin your Day One.

WEEK 16

"Never underestimate the importance of the beginning."

Carolyn Coman

START SOMETHING

"Are you sure you're ready to make this move? It's a big risk to be taking right now, especially since we're in the middle of a recession," my friend said, after I told him my plans to leave my day job.

"I know," I said, not really sure about what to say next. Even though I knew he was only trying to help, I didn't want to say anything that could make him think that I had any doubts about my decision.

"What about your kids and Dede? I mean, its great if you make it, but where will it leave you guys if you don't?" he asked.

"Listen, I don't have all the answers. All I know is that if I don't make a move now, I may never do it. And for me, the only thing worse than failing, is knowing you have the potential to be great at something but refuse to try. This is my shot. There's no other choice but to take it," I said.

I couldn't tell you how many times I parked in that parking structure or walked through the doors and turned my computer on in my office; but this time, as much as I loved working there and all of the great memories that were made, and the people I met, I knew I needed to close the door on this chapter of my life. I needed to start with the new me and make a transition.

Only a few people understood why it was so important for me to leave a stable job and go out and do what I was created to do - inspire people and help them raise their level of thinking and encourage them to tap into their

Greatness. The question is, why did it take so long to do what I wanted to do? The biggest issue for me was timing - I was afraid that if I left too early, I might jeopardize my family's well being. I knew I was skilled enough and felt pumped enough, but I felt trapped in professional quicksand. But then one day, it hit me, "It's now or never." And with that, I made the necessary moves to end one career and start my future.

> The biggest issue for me was timing - I was afraid that if I left too early, I might jeopardize my family's well being.

DAY ONE: LEARN IT

New beginnings are scary - I've had enough to know. Maybe you're thinking about going back to school, opening a new business, or starting a new relationship. You don't reach the top of the mountain from the top of the mountain. At some point, there was a bottom... there was a climb... there was a struggle and that first step up the mountain was the most important step because, without it, you'd still be at the bottom. In fact, I've learned that the only thing better than taking that first step, is being at the top and looking back on your journey. What mountain can you commit to climbing today?

> You don't reach the top of the mountain from the top of the mountain.

Create a realistic timeline that will identify the process from when you take your first step toward climbing your mountain to the day/event that will signify that you have made it to the top of your mountain. An example from my life would be a timeline showing the day that I filled out the application to take the GED course (my first step), and then every step leading up to me walking across the stage to accept my PhD (the top of my mountain).

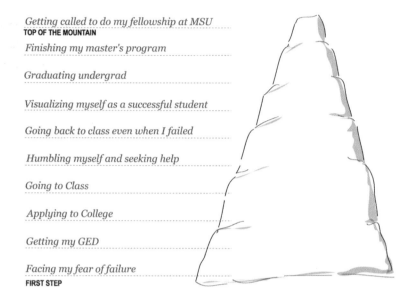

Getting called to do my fellowship at MSU
TOP OF THE MOUNTAIN

Finishing my master's program

Graduating undergrad

Visualizing myself as a successful student

Going back to class even when I failed

Humbling myself and seeking help

Going to Class

Applying to College

Getting my GED

Facing my fear of failure
FIRST STEP

Challenge

What first step do you need to take?

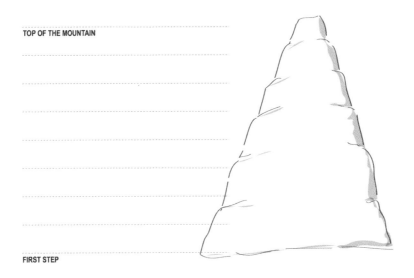

TOP OF THE MOUNTAIN

FIRST STEP

DAY TWO: ACCEPT IT

It takes longer than a day or even a week to get started on a new endeavor. But this week, I'm going to get you going in the right direction. What is the one thing in your life that if you had no fears (i.e., no financial concerns, no ties, no restrictions, etc.) you would start on it right away?

_____

_____

_____

CHALLENGE

Write that challenge here:
I accept the fact that I haven't named my mountain. Today, I will take the first step and name my Mountain:

_____

I promise myself that I will do

_____

and be

_____

DAY THREE: EMBRACE IT

You may be thinking, ET, why are you so adamant about research. Its simple - information is the gateway to success. It's cliche, but you can't grow if you don't know. I research everything. I research my interests; I research my competition; and I do research on how to research. Why? Because that's how you advance to the next level.

Research the mountain that you described on Day Two. For example, maybe you've always wanted to start your own business, but you were turned off by the costs of starting a new company, or maybe you're afraid to take the risk because you already have a full-time job. Whatever endeavor you've been wanting to start, begin the research on it today. What costs are associated with it? What other people (in your life or in the media) have been successful at this endeavor? How long does it take? What is the process to get started? Write the answers to these questions down in your GIUY Success Journal.

DAY FOUR: CHANGE IT

Many people want to start something new in their life but have no idea where to begin. Here's some help:

Get rid of "Stinking Thinking."

We've already discussed how negative thinking adversely impacts your outcome. It is the biggest hinderance to moving in to an unchartered territory. Replace thoughts like, "I'm afraid," "I can't," "It won't work because…" with "I can do it," "I Will do it," and "I MUST do it."

Take ownership for your actions.

Remember the Victim vs. Victor's mentality from earlier? The only way you will be able to successfully start something new is if you are in a place in your life where you are ready to deal with the consequences. If you're going to blame others for your failed attempts, then it's better to wait until you've progressed to this level.

Take advantage of an opportunity of a lifetime in the lifetime of the opportunity.

Remember, there are some things that you just don't have forever to make a move on. I knew that if I didn't leave my office job when I did, that "Life" would continue to happen and before I knew it, the opportunity to live my dream would have been gone.

Leave the Lurker's mindset behind

Complacency is the one guaranteed way to NOT start something new in your life. If you're already comfortable with where you are, chances are that you aren't trying to do anything different. Similarly, waiting on others to give you a chance to start your new endeavor is just as inhibiting to a new start.

Ask the Guru

Do you want to know how that single mom got up the nerve to go back to school? Do you want to know how your boss secured his position with the company in just a few years? Are you curious about how your neighbor started his own company? Ask them how they got started. This is possibly the biggest first step you can make in starting your new journey - getting the information.

Now that you have some information to help you get started, how will you implement these five steps to help you make that big change in your life?

_____

_____

_____

What additional things can you do to help you start your new endeavor?

_____

_____

_____

DAY FIVE: LIVE IT

Today, you set your climb in action by taking the 1st step. In your research on Day Three, you were asked to learn the necessary process for achieving your goal. For instance, if your mountain involves going to school or joining the service, you might have learned in your research that there is an application process. If this is the case, print and fill out the application today. The very first step you take should be the first step you listed on your timeline. Create your 7-day plan to make your new beginning.

SUNDAY   *i.e., Write my 7-day plan ...*
_____

_____

*Use your GIUY Success Journal to write out your plan.

GREATNESS IS...

Innovation.

Love them or hate them, everyone knows the name Ford. Henry Ford didn't invent the automobile. He wasn't even responsible for the first assembly line, but what he did to change the game was that he was brave enough to step out and take chance after chance after chance at something he had never done before and he took it and revolutionized the industry. He was fired from his first job and his first two companies were failures, but he kept moving in the direction of his mountain.

Listen, sometimes that first step you take might set you back two or three more steps, but you've got to make up in your mind that you're ok with the consequences. Something inside of you has to value the process more than the temporary upsets.

There are a million motivational speakers and coaches in this industry, the odds were against me before I even delivered my first speech, but I knew that if I could just keep my eyes on the peak of the mountain... though the winds were rising steadily against me and a thousand obstacles stood in my way, I was anchored... steadfast... unmovable... unshakeable... I knew that there was something for me if I just allowed myself to move with the currents.

And the reason that many people will never see the top of their mountains, is because they become so paralyzed by the fear of not making it past the first step.

Greatness is saying, "Yes, I am afraid of failing, but I'm more afraid of failing to try."

Spend time today reflecting on your actions this week.

Did you meet the challenge? If not, why?

_____

_____

SUMMARY OF THE WEEK

You don't reach the top of the mountain from the top of the mountain.

WHAT MOUNTAIN CAN YOU COMMIT TO
CLIMBING

What is the one thing in your life that if you had no fears you would start on it right away?

RESEARCH
information is the gateway to success

Create a realistic
TIMELINE

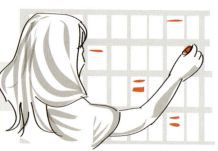

TAKE THE FIRST STEPS

- Get rid of "Stinking Thinking"
- Take ownership of your actions
- Take advantage of an opportunity of a lifetime in the lifetime of the opportunity
- Leave the Lurker's mindset behind
- Ask the Guru

GREATNESS IS UPON YOU
CERTIFICATE OF COMPLETION

This is to certify that

_____

has successfully completed this week's challenge.

Eric Thomas and Associates, LLC

_____
signature

_____
date

WEEK

17

WORDS OF GREATNESS

EXTINGUISH
to put an end to or bring to an end

FUEL
something that gives nourishment

EXTINGUISHING THE FIRE VS. FUELING THE FIRE

Are you fueling your flames or letting them die out?

It's frustrating for many people to set goals for themselves and then look back on them years later just to find their goals incomplete. What is the common denominator to our unsuccessful endeavors? This week we investigate how factors external to your goal affect your ability to achieve desired outcomes.

WEEK 17

"We begin to see, therefore, the importance of selecting our environment with the greatest of care, because environment is the mental feeding ground out of which the food that goes into our minds is extracted."

Napoleon Hill

EXTREME MAKEOVER

"I've been trying to lose the same 80lbs for the last 6 years, and I'm not getting anywhere."

These were the frustrated sentiments of LaShanna, the Director of Operations of our team.

As we're talking, she says, "E, I'm telling you, I'm done. I've been up and down with my weight loss, and I'm thinking that there isn't any hope."

"There's always hope, L. But let me ask you, what kind of things are you doing to lose weight?" I asked.

"I'm not one of those people who says they're on a diet, but then you catch them at the Super Buffet going in for round 6 on the orange chicken and shrimp fried rice," she replied. "I honestly have put forth my best effort and have tried literally every diet program on the planet. I've done hormone drops, appetite suppressants, Zumba, gym memberships, meal replacements, fasts... I even tried the *Pray your hunger pains away diet*, where every time you feel hungry, you say a prayer...I prayed a lot and I gained 5lbs...trust me, nothing works."

I knew that even though she was partly joking, she was dead serious. I've seen her commit to several diets over the years that I've known her and, while it was true that she wasn't getting the results that she wanted, I knew that there was something else missing. It wasn't that her weight loss was up and down (although it was true); it was that she was having trouble with consistency. Different factors in her environment would cause her to breach her contract to weight loss.

So I asked her, "Do the things you surround yourself with speak to the goal you're trying to accomplish?"

"No disrespect, E," she began to cry, "but I don't need a motivational speaker right now. It's like I told you, I have tried everything I can think of, and with all the money that I've spent on diets, I could've paid for 3 gastric surgeries by now. I don't need a speech. I just need your support. I walk into stores and sales people look at me sideways, because I can't fit into the clothes on their racks, and they wonder why I even came through the door in the first place. I avoid going to theme parks with my friends, because I can't take the embarrassment of being asked to get off the ride. I cover myself with a blanket on the airplane, so people won't see that I can't buckle my seat belt. I get up some mornings and I have to force myself out of bed. I cling to the sheets, because I don't want to face a world where people judge your abilities based on how quickly you can get up a flight of stairs.

I watch people around me, some smaller and some larger, lose weight. And I'm jealous. I'm not lazy, and I'm not trying to push a sob story. I'm telling you that it's hard and I'm tired."

I understood her pain. And she cried it out a little longer and I gave her the ear that she needed.

The next day, I called to check on her, and she assured me that she was doing better. We talked a little more about her challenges with committing to her weight loss and the things that were working against her to kill her ability to be consistent. By her own admission, she would get weary of different programs when she didn't immediately see the results she was looking for and became easily deterred when certain things changed in her environment.

"You've set the goal and you've got the desire, but are you placing yourself in an environment that will allow you to support your weight loss goals?" I asked. "What are the eating habits of the people you surround yourself with? What type of music are you listening to when you work out? What kind of conversations are you having about food? What type of books are you reading? Believe it or not, the things in your environment make a difference," I said.

I explained to her my own weight loss journey and how I lost almost 50lbs since the recording of my first YouTube video about the Guru Story. I explained to her that I literally had to change my environment in order to get the results that I needed because, like her, I was up and down with my commitment to weight loss. But one day, I was out to dinner with my family, and I noticed that I had gotten a DM on my Twitter account from someone who had been watching the videos and wondered how I could be so passionate in my messages about success but not use that same energy towards my weight loss. It only took a few seconds to read that message, but it felt like a lifetime as I looked at the table of food that was sitting in front of me and my family.

> You can't expect an addict to recover from his addiction in an atmosphere that supports or feeds the addiction.

I began to think about the way that I talked about food and I realized that it all had to change. So not only did I get back into the gym after that message, but I refinished my basement so that I could have certain things that would stimulate me while I worked out from home. I purchased the bikes first and then got surround sound for my stereo and TV equipment. I kept the temperature in the basement chilled so that I could be more comfortable. Then I purchased two treadmills (one for me and one for my wife so that she could work out as well and become my accountability partner). I bought a juicer and a deep freezer so that I can have fruit and vegetables at any point in the day. I removed all of the junk food from our cabinets and I became more aware of the foods that would reinforce and support my own weight loss goals.

My point is that many people try to do different things or become better as a person without changing their environment. You can't expect an addict to recover from his addiction in an atmosphere that supports or feeds the addiction. The chances of being able to commit to recovery are slim even with the best intentions. Similarly, you can't expect to change an aspect of your life without being willing to look at how external factors are hindering or supporting your change.

DAY ONE: LEARN IT

> We all want to make changes in our lives in some aspect

We all want to make changes in our lives in some aspect and, like LaShanna, we have tried various means to meet our objectives but have fallen short; not because we didn't put forth the effort, but because there were things that were external to our goals that discouraged our consistency or that worked to extinguish our fire.

Fire needs three things to keep it going: heat, fuel, and oxygen. Heat is necessary to ignite the fire and help it to spread; the fuel is any combustible material; and the oxygen supports the reaction. If any one of the three elements is eliminated, then the fire is extinguished.

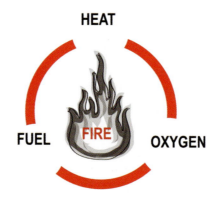

Fig. 1. Elements needed to keep a fire burning.

Theoretically, how could we apply this same triangle to the fires we have in our own lives? Let's consider the story about LaShanna. Remember, she admitted to struggling for years with her weight. There were times when she was up and times when she was down, but she was never able to keep her momentum going and, thus, never met her weight loss goal. Why wasn't she able to keep her fire going?

Remember, to maintain a fire, you need a combination of heat, fuel, and oxygen. Consistency also requires a trio: a goal, desire, and support.

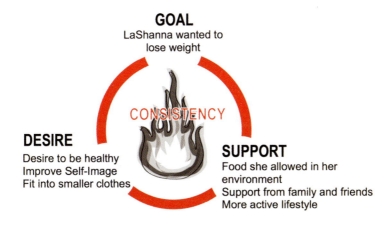

Fig. 2. Real life example.

Recall that if we were to remove any one of the three elements that the fire would be extinguished. This means that if weight loss was no longer a goal for LaShanna or if she no longer desired to improve her self-image, the fire would be extinguished. Similarly, if she removed healthy foods from her environment or became less active, her fire (i.e., her consistency) would burn out and thus her goal of losing weight would be compromised.

Becoming Phenomenal means not letting Life's inconsistencies make you inconsistent in achieving the goals that you've set for yourself.

On the other hand, any unknown health issues aside, if LaShanna had a continued interest in her weight loss combined with the desire to be healthy and improve her self-image, and if she also remained active and restricted herself to a healthier diet, the fire would continue to burn.

While we've noted that all three factors are essential in keeping the flames going, many people take for granted how important the third element, **Support** or Environmental influences are on our ability to be consistent. For the most part, when we've set a goal, we still want that goal to be met, and whatever other desires that originally fueled our flames are still there in some form or another, but the hardest thing to keep in tact is the support; it is the most unstable of the other three elements and thus the hardest to control.

This means that LaShanna could do everything in her power to keep all three parts of the triangle in tact, but the minute something happened in her environment that she couldn't control (i.e., surprise birthday party, a new job that required her to travel and eat out a lot) the longevity of her fire (or ability to be consistent) would be in jeopardy UNLESS she became skilled at forecasting and protecting against those potential hazards in her environment that could throw her off her game.

This is what happens to many of us when we seek out new endeavors.

Becoming Great means not letting life's inconsistencies make you inconsistent in achieving the goals that you've set for yourself.

What Extinguishing Fire factors are prevalent in your life? List them in your GIUY Success Journal.

_____

_____

_____

DAY TWO: ACCEPT IT

GOAL

All of us have experienced at least one occasion in our life where we set out to make some improvement to ourself or in our life but failed to actually follow through on it. Perhaps you wanted to quit a bad habit but haven't been able to stop yet, or maybe you wanted to network more and meet more people in your field of interest, but you still shy away from public events.

List 3 areas in your life where you set a goal but have proven up to this point in your life to be unsuccessful in meeting it.

i.e., Building stronger outreach programs within my company.

1. _____

2. _____

3. _____

Take one of the areas that you identified and think of 3-5 things that you can do to reignite that fire!

1. _____

2. _____

3. _____

DAY THREE: EMBRACE IT
DESIRE

Let's keep it real, sometimes it's hard to self-motivate and we need some help keeping coals on the fire. This is ok. When "Life" happens, it's only normal to temporarily forget why we've set the goals we've set. If we're no longer excited, the fire dies. When you're low on ammunition, who will you call to keep the embers going? Who holds you accountable?

Describe what "Fueling your fire" skills your friends possess and how you specifically plan to call on these skills. Identify what times in your life you will need to call on them.

_____

_____

DAY FOUR: CHANGE IT
SUPPORT

Today, we're going to get you prepared for potential unforeseen events. In college, to prepare students for the real world, professors advise students to do a Mock Interview. Why? So that they can experience the process before it happens. Today, you are going to create an experience that would ordinarily alter your environment (i.e., a scenario where you feel stressed, discouraged, unmotivated, or where things or people you were trying to eliminate have somehow reappeared, etc.) and role play how you will reset your atmosphere (i.e., read a poem, play some music, review your goal list, etc.).

Protecting your environment is essential to your cause.

Protect: What can you do to build a more stable environment for the goal(s) that you've set?

Forecast: What are the potential threats?

DAY FIVE: LIVE IT

Don't get caught off guard - stay ahead of the game. Create a 7-day plan for how you will make the needed adjustments to your environment to help you stay consistent.

SUNDAY   *i.e., Write my 7-day plan ...*

*Use your GIUY Success Journal to write out your plan.

Greatness Is...

Remember the story of the Rabbit and the Turtle?

The Rabbit was bragging about how fast he was, and the Turtle challenges him to a race. Everything about the Rabbit said that he should have won this race, he was stronger and faster and, let's face it, he was going up against a turtle! Why wouldn't he win? Yet, he didn't. And this was a great disappointment; but the only thing that cost him the race - was him.

The thing that destroyed the Rabbit's success wasn't his confidence in his abilities, it wasn't his intellect, and it wasn't that the turtle had some super natural gift. The goal had been set, he had the desire to win, and everyone in his environment believed that he would do it, but then he decided to stop and take a nap. He sabotaged his own success by killing his fire, because even though it was only for a few minutes, he no longer desired to keep running. And those minutes cost him everything.

Think about what one day of not working out does to your weight loss goal; what one day of not doing your homework does to your goal of getting your diploma or degree. What does one day of not writing a page in your book do to your momentum?

The Rabbit killed his own momentum by stopping - he wasn't consistent.

Consistency is the powerhouse of every successful endeavor. I'm not saying it's easy, but it is necessary if you want to see yourself move to the next level.

> Greatness is resisting the temptation to throw in the towel even when everything in your environment says you should.

Spend time today reflecting on your actions this week.

Did you meet the challenge? If not, why?

SUMMARY OF THE WEEK

FIRE NEEDS THREE THINGS TO KEEP IT GOING

 **VS**

EXTINGUISHING YOUR FIRE VS **FUELING YOUR FIRE**

  **CALL A FRIEND**

FORTIFY YOUR ENVIRONMENT

IDENTIFY WHAT TIMES IN YOUR LIFE YOU WILL NEED TO CALL

ROLE PLAY HOW TO RESET YOUR ATMOSPHERE

GREATNESS IS UPON YOU
CERTIFICATE OF COMPLETION

This is to certify that

_____

has successfully completed this week's challenge.

Eric Thomas and Associates, LLC

_____
signature

_____
date

WEEK 18

WORDS OF GREATNESS

CREATE
to cause to come into being, as something unique that would not naturally evolve or that is not made by ordinary processes

LOST IN GRIEF VS. WORKING THROUGH PAIN

Do you allow yourself to get lost in grief or do you find a way to push through it?

There are a few chapters that I've set aside to discuss setbacks and how we should handle them. It's a complicated topic and people often want to know what I mean when I say that I'm grateful for my pain. This week we discuss the first step for using your pain to push you to Greatness - getting through it.

WEEK 18

"Even in death, there is beauty"

Eric Thomas

CREATE BEAUTY FROM DEATH

It was quiet. The hospital room was full of conflicting emotions - fear, sadness, disbelief, anger, and surprisingly, peace. The doctors had already told us that she could go at any minute. I looked over at MaBez, who only months earlier was vibrant and full of life, but now laid decrepit, quivering, and weak. She motioned for me to walk over to her bed and take her hand.

No one said a word but a brief survey of her loved ones revealed solemn tear stained faces full of sorrow and grief. But MaBez's face, though small and still, revealed eyes that danced with contentment and joy.

I met her through my pastor, Dr. James Doggett, at a speaking engagement during my earlier days and almost instantly, we connected as friends. She was my spiritual mom and introduced me to *The Prayer of Jabez,* which ultimately taught me what I call the Jabez aspect of my Christian faith - being a servant. She was the one who taught me the true importance of service and helped me to understand the art to giving phenomenally. Through the years, our families became very close. She was another grandma to my children and an inspiration to my wife and mom.

Her health began to fail her during one of the highest traveling periods of my life. I looked for ways to arrange for me and my family to make it to her side, but ultimatelyI had to rely on God to create a miracle for me to spend time with her during her final hours. As her thumb rubbed back and forth against the back of my hand, a number of thoughts ran through my mind as I thought of our relationship and the impact she had on me and my family. The room was so silent, but I was so restricted by my grief that I couldn't think of anything to say.

I opened my mouth to say a prayer but then, as if MaBez was reading my mind, she began to sing in the faintest voice, *"Lord, I will lift... mine eyes to the hills. Knowing my help is coming from You. Your peace you give me, in time of a storm... ."*

My wife grabbed my other hand as tears began to form in my own eyes. She continued to sing with what could only be described as joy. *"You are the source of my strength. You are the strength of my life. I lift my hands in Total Praise to you."* Even in her last hours MaBez was singing and praising God.

Watching her slip away was one of the greatest tragedies and joys I've ever experienced.

It seems odd to use the word "joy" when you're watching someone you love pass away, but there was such peace and comfort in her final days that seeing her enwrapped in what was becoming the emergence of a new life created a sensation that can only be described as Joy. And though I miss her terribly, the impact that she had on my life and the life of my family and the thousands of other lives she touched, is the type of immortal beauty that artists starve themselves to capture in their paintings. It would almost be selfish of me to see her passing as anything less than that.

DAY ONE: LEARN IT

In later chapters we will discuss the importance of making the best of hardships, resilience, and how having a vision helps you to move past many of the setbacks that life can bring. This week, the emphasis is simply on finding light in the midst of your darkness - identifying the positive in the negative and working through it.

Right now, you may be experiencing some hardships (or the aftermath of some hardships). Perhaps you're recently divorced, or lost a loved one... or maybe you feel like everything you touch is a failure, and you don't know which way to go. Just remember that the darkest moment in the night is when the sun begins to rise.

Working through your crisis may require a little time, but you can move past the pain. I've endured several painful losses in my life. Here are some useful techniques that I had to learn to push me past my pain.

Learn It.

Ask other people who have had similar experiences about strategies they used to work through their pain. But you're not limited to just the people in your immediate circle, there is a mountain of resources out there to consult about your specific situation - the more you know about your hardship, the better you'll be able to cope with it. For me, listening to other people's testimony about how they successfully got through their darker moments gave me a framework to work from.

Accept It.

Acceptance is hard for many people, but it's possibly the most essential part of recovery. It's important to not only accept that the devastation has happened, but it's equally important to accept whatever support is offered to you by your family and friends.

I was able to spend time with MaBez in her last days so acceptance of her death was a little easier for me than it may have otherwise been. I believe the trickiest part is allowing yourself to be vulnerable enough to accept the support (i.e., loving comments, efforts, etc.,) of others. Devastation can make us want to isolate from others. Some people shut out friends and family. Others bury themselves in work or projects. This is a mistake. Remember in the previous chapter, we discussed how eliminating support can keep you from meeting your goals. The same still applies here, when you refuse to accept support, you create an opportunity to get lost in your pain instead of creating an opportunity to move past it. It is the most counterproductive thing you can do to your recovery.

Embrace It.

Many people make the mistake of thinking that they can run from the pain. They drown themselves in drugs, alcohol, or other harmful behavior, so that they won't have to feel the hurt. Dealing with your pain requires you to first embrace the fact that it exists, meaning, allow yourself to experience all of the pain that the devastation created. If you need to cry, then cry. If you have to scream or yell, then do that. Don't be afraid to live out the extent of your grief. When I first learned that my friend was only given a few days to live, it shook me. There were moments when I didn't want to even think about it- all I wanted to do was work. But I allowed myself to go through the motions, because I knew they were necessary in order for me to get to the next phase.

Change It.

When you've gone through steps 1-3, the only thing left is to change it - allow your setback to be the setup for a comeback. We discuss the different ways to do this in subsequent chapters, but to start you must find the positive in the negative. What can you take from the experience to create a new, more meaningful experience? Sometimes the answer isn't always obvious. I began by submerging myself in inspiration from as many avenues as possible - books, online sources, friends, and family and I let their words fuel me until I'm in a place to fuel myself.

Many people have heard me talk about how I used my pain to push me to Greatness. The fact is, I had to go through each of these steps to get me to that place. If I never tried to understand what was happening in my life; if I never accepted it; if I never embraced it; I would have never gotten to the part where I got to change it - channel my pain into something productive.

DAY TWO: ACCEPT IT

Explore your creative gene. Today, I want you to express your feelings about your hardships creatively. Even if you're not an artist, there are artistic ways to express yourself, and many times the expression of art can be therapeutic. You can prepare for your journey this week by writing a poem, lyrics to a song, a painting, etc. Feel free to be you.

DAY THREE: EMBRACE IT

It's hard when we feel like we're the only ones struggling through something. But the reality is that everyone is going through a hardship, whether they make it known to you or not. Sometimes the recovery process is expedited when we help others who are experiencing their own challenges.

Today, move out of your comfort zone and help someone you know who is going through hardships. When I lost my friend, I found a lot of solace in catering to the needs of some of my other loved ones who were experiencing their own hardships. What can you do for a family member, friend, or colleague today?

DAY FOUR: CHANGE IT

Exercise is a great way to get your mind off things and to lift your spirits. My morning runs were a lot more intense when I was grieving the loss of my friend. I channeled what I was feeling into my morning routines.

Even if you're presently active in an exercise regimen, sometimes it pays to give your body a break from the ordinary and treat it to something new.

Commit to a new workout activity today. Run an extra mile, try the elliptical instead of the treadmill, take a spin class, join a Zumba class, or simply change sceneries and walk at a different park. Whatever you do, make it active, and allow yourself to burn away the sadness and enjoy the energetic rush!

As you are working out, think through what new meaningful experience can be created through your loss.

Identify it in your GIUY Success Journal:

_____

_____

_____

_____

DAY FIVE: LIVE IT

The goal is to find the Beauty in your Loss. Create a 7-day plan that you can commit to to help you begin the move past your pain.

SUNDAY   *i.e., Write my 7-day plan ...*
_____

*Use your GIUY Success Journal to write out your plan.

Greatness Is...

Imagine waking up to what seems like a normal day. You get up and open your blinds to see the sunrise from your bedroom patio and there isn't a cloud in the sky. You reach for your morning cup of coffee when suddenly the phone rings; it's your broker calling to tell you that the market crashed, and you've lost all of your assets. You're arguing with your broker about how this could possibly happen considering the flawless portfolio he showed you yesterday. As he begins to move into an explanation, your other line begins to <<beep>>. You click over to hear your lawyer tell you that the property you just closed on was illegally obtained, and not only did you have to stop all plans to break ground for the new shopping mall, you just hired dozens of contractors to build; but the guy who sold you the property is nowhere to be found. Practically numb from what could only be described as the trailer to the movie, The Worst Day Ever, *you get a knock at the door and, eager for even the slightest bit of relief, you run down the stairs to answer the door and find a police officer standing in your doorway. Confused, you ask him to come in. He enters apologizing, explaining to you that your family was the fourth car in a twenty car pile up on the Interstate and, unfortunately, there were no survivors.*

Extreme? Maybe. But my point is that devastation can strike at any moment.

The reason I love the story of Job so much is because it exemplifies for me the mentality we all should have when we've suffered a loss. Job had everything. And without warning, it was all gone. He lost his riches, his children were murdered, he became severely ill, and his wife lost faith in his beliefs. Through his anguish, depression, and heartache, he never denied the one thing that sustained him. He said, "The Lord giveth and the Lord taketh away. Blessed be the name of the Lord." I've lost everyone and everything that ever mattered to me but, "Blessed be the name of the Lord." I've worked hard and done everything I was supposed to do but, "Blessed be the name of the Lord." My friends don't understand me but, "Blessed be the name of the Lord." My wife has turned her back on me but, "Blessed be the name of the Lord." My enemies rejoice in their iniquities while I have lived a pure and righteous life but, "Blessed be the name of the Lord." I feel broken, defeated, and full of despair but, "Blessed be the name of the Lord."

Greatness is making a decision. Greatness is deciding that darkness is darkness, but darkness will not destroy you. Greatness is not letting your agony consume you and getting through it all with your integrity intact.

Many of us have been devastated by sudden or even anticipated tragedies. But you have to learn to go through pain (in whatever form it is presented to you) without allowing it to break your spirit. No one gets excited about the dark moments when they hit, but the Greats use tragedies to their advantage. Even in the midst of catastrophic adversity, Job didn't succumb to the pressure that his wounds had stacked against him, he was beaten but he didn't break.

Greatness is remembering in the dark what God told you in the light.

Spend time today reflecting on your actions this week.

Did you meet the challenge? If not, why?

_____

_____

_____

_____

_____

_____

_____

_____

SUMMARY OF THE WEEK

MOVE PAST THE PAIN
CHANGE IT
EMBRACE IT
ACCEPT IT
LEARN IT

EXPRESS YOUR FEELING ABOUT YOUR HARDSHIPS
CREATIVELY
by writing a poem, lyrics to a song, a painting, etc.

HELP

HELP SOMEONE THAT YOU KNOW WHO IS GOING THROUGH HARDSHIPS

COMMIT TO A NEW
NEW WORKOUT
enjoy the energetic rush!

GREATNESS IS UPON YOU
CERTIFICATE OF COMPLETION

This is to certify that

_____

has successfully completed this week's challenge.

Eric Thomas and Associates, LLC

_____
signature

_____
date

WEEK

19

WORDS OF GREATNESS

ALL
the whole of; the greatest possible

"SOMETIMES", "MAYBE", "I'M NOT SURE" VS. 120% "ALL IN"

Are you tapped out at 80% or are you "ALL IN"?

In chapter 18, we talked about why it's important to be consistent Lets take it a step further and explore not just the need to be consistent but to consistently give 120% in everything that we do.

WEEK 19

"I bring my 'A' game everyday because its the only game I have."

Eric Thomas

BRING YOUR "A" GAME

"Mr. Thomas?" the lady on the other end of the phone asked, a little puzzled.

"Yes, this is him," I said with a half grin on my face. Even though I knew she was talking about me, it was funny to hear anybody call me *Mr. Thomas*. Mr. Thomas is my dad.

"Mr. Thomas, this is Nadlie calling in regards to your speaking engagement with our company tomorrow morning. We're all really excited here in the office. We've taken the liberty of showing your videos to some of our top and most influential leaders, and they will be present for your presentation tomorrow morning," she said in a what I could only perceive to be a *you've been warned* kind of voice.

The next day, a few of my team members and I get to the office out on the east coast, and I was approached by a gentleman wearing a navy blue tailored fit suit. Now, my team and I wear our Grind Gear apparel everywhere we go to promote the brand and our message; I guess this must have thrown the guy in the navy blue suit off because he pulled me to the side and said, "Mr. Thomas," *there was that name again*, "Mr. Thomas, I need you to understand the depth of this engagement. I don't know who you've worked with before, but this is next level."

It was difficult not to laugh to myself a little. You could tell that he was one of those guys who made everything seem super urgent and today was no different. "Ok, talk to me," I said.

"We're bringing down our top leaders, so they're not going to be on the phones. This means that we're going to potentially be losing thousands of dollars in that hour we're working with you. So you have to…when this is over, you have to produce. Mr. Thomas," he said, placing his hand on my shoulder, "I'm going to need your 'A' game."

"My 'A' game," I said, nodding.

Unbelievable. I thought to myself as he continued to speak. I respected where he was coming from, but his statement let me know that he had no idea who I was or where I came from.

Apparently, in his world, you could bring multiple games - "A," "B," and "C." But my mom got pregnant when she was 17 and I didn't establish a relationship with my real father until I was 30; my son did something that neither me, my father, or grandfather was able to do - break the cycle of being a high school drop; and I have a daughter who wants to go to Harvard.

He didn't get it, I bring my "A" game to every event I go to - I don't have a choice. I don't get to choose. I don't have a "B" game or a "C" game, because when I speak, too many people are depending on me. So I bring my "A" game to every seminar, every session, and every workshop, because it's the only game I've got.

So many people forget where they came from and what they went through to get where they are. They forget what it was like when they were hustling to make it through college or fighting to get out of a bad neighborhood.

You might be sweeter than me. You might be bigger than me. You might have more money and more resources, but you will not outwork me. This is my mindset. Most of us only get one shot, and I can't miss mine because I chose to give less than what I'm capable of giving. And neither can you.

If you're not willing to go All In and give 120% every single time, then you might as well clock out and let the next man clock in and prove his worth.

DAY ONE: LEARN IT

What's the difference between an "A" game and any other game? It's the difference between being under contract and being in a covenant relationship.

A contract is a legal document that binds two or more parties. Before it's drafted, the terms of the contract are negotiated. Each side decides what they are willing to give and take and the document itself, is often riddled with loop-holes and "get-out" clauses; in short, they are written to be broken.

A covenant, on the other hand, is an agreement made under oath, upheld through a person's actions, and is considered to be binding for all time - no negotiating; no loopholes; no outs. It's a more sacred form of union that says plain and simply, "Yes. I'm all in."

Are you "All In" or are you making excuses and operating from a contract mindset? Meaning, you only give how much you want when the terms are right and you're ready to back out at any time.

A million different things can get in the way of our being able to give 120%. Conflicting schedules, time management issues, laziness, family life, misunderstandings, financial challenges, and the list continues. And sometimes we simply want to see how little we can do and still reap the biggest possible reward.

But even in the midst of these obstacles, we owe it to ourselves and the people who depend on us to represent the 120 in all that we do consistently because every moment counts.

What challenges or obstacles do you face that actively inhibit your ability to go ALL IN? In these areas of your life, have you proven yourself to be one who gets discouraged and quits (under contract), or have you proven yourself to be one who picks up the pieces and recreates destiny (lives by covenant)?

DAY TWO: ACCEPT IT

CONTRACT

I accept the fact that I am not consistent in bringing my "A" game everyday.

I allow the following factors to inhibit me from doing my best:

_____

_____

_____

_____

_____

_____

_____

_____

DAY THREE: EMBRACE IT

Remember, covenants are promises that are meant to bind you for life - there are no termination clauses. What aspects of your life are you willing to make a covenant with? Keep in mind that this means that you are consistently giving 120% effort. Fill in the blanks below:

I vow to give 120% to be All In in spite of the fact that

_____

_____

even when my haters

_____

_____

and when the circumstances are not quite

_____

_____

DAY FOUR: CHANGE IT

Let's identify all of the times that you don't go ALL IN (bring your "A" game), and then identify the patterns you notice in each situation. What personal reasons do you have for not showing up consistently and giving your all in every aspect. (i.e., lack passion, little to no direction, complacency, etc.)?

If you didn't make the changes in this area of your life, who would you be letting down and why?

Examples:

I get poor grades on exams all the time. I notice that before every exam, I get really anxious because I'm afraid I'm going to fail. But if I don't find a way to channel my anxiety, I could lose my scholarship and all of my hard work will have been in vain.

I am late to work every Monday. I notice that I have a hard time getting up on time after the weekend, because I dread the work week. But if I continue to go to work late, I could lose my job and this would be bad for my family, because they depend on me.

DAY FIVE: LIVE IT

We've already discussed how consistency is a key factor in your ability to be successful. What can you do to make sure that you consistently bring your "A" game to every endeavor? Develop your 7-day plan to get the most out of yourself.

SUNDAY   *i.e., Write my 7-day plan ...*
_____

_____

*Use your GIUY Success Journal to write out your plan.

Greatness Is...

There's a popular illustration of two men digging for diamonds. In the illustration, the guy on the top is hammering away to get to the diamonds, but you can tell that he still has a ways to go. Meanwhile, the guy on the bottom, has stopped hammering and is walking in the opposite direction of the diamonds and, from the illustration, you can tell that if he had just given the gravel one or two more whacks with his hammer, the diamonds would have all come rushing out.

I've seen people use this illustration as an example of why we should never give up. But what if the guy at the bottom didn't intend to give up and was simply tired from all of the hammering he had been doing? So instead of hammering away at full speed, he decided to relax and take a break? The results are still the same. Whether you give up completely or you decide to just give 60% effort one day out of 7 days, you risk missing out on collecting diamonds. Is this a risk you're willing to take?

Consistency is not your burden. Actually, it is the one thing that can effectively alleviate any burdens you may have.

In Biblical times, covenants were considered sacred, because it signified a promise that would never be broken. There are certain disappointments that will prove to be inevitable simply because we're expecting a covenant relationship but putting in contract effort.

Greatness is the end result of consistency backed by an unbreachable promise.

Spend time today reflecting on your actions this week.

Did you meet the challenge? If not, why?

_____

_____

_____

SUMMARY OF THE WEEK

ARE YOU "ALL IN"?

BEING UNDER CONTRACT
written to be broken

BEING UNDER COVENANT
120% committed

What aspects of your life are you willing to make a covenant with ?

IDENTIFY

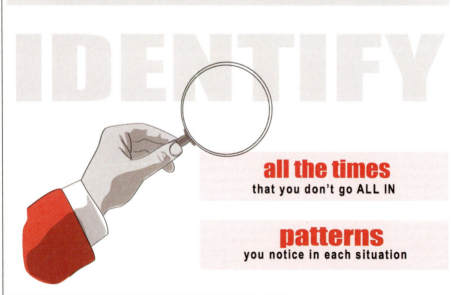

all the times
that you don't go ALL IN

patterns
you notice in each situation

GREATNESS IS UPON YOU
CERTIFICATE OF COMPLETION

This is to certify that

_____

has successfully completed this week's challenge.

Eric Thomas and Associates, LLC

_____
signature

_____
date

WEEK

20

WORDS OF GREATNESS

PERSEVERE
to maintain a purpose in spite of difficulty, obstacles, or discouragement

BEATEN VS. BESTED

Are setbacks merely setbacks for you or an opportunity for a comeback?

Adversities, disappointments, setbacks, hardships... all of these things are a part of life. But just because you can't avoid the hard stuff, doesn't mean you should let it beat you. In Week 18, we talked about grief. This week, we look at examples of people who have made misfortune work in their favor, and discuss how you can do the same.

WEEK 20

"Don't get bitter...get better."

A lot of people...

TURN LEMONS INTO LEMONADE

I heard it, but I couldn't believe it. It was all over the news, so I already knew it was an incredible story, but listening to the actual 911 call of Antoinette Tuff talking down the Atlanta gunman was one of the few moments that left me speechless.

"It's going to be alright, sweetie," she tells the gunman.

"I just want you to know I love you, though, OK? And I'm proud of you. That's a good thing that you're just giving up, and don't worry about it. We all go through something in life. I thought the same thing, you know, I tried to commit suicide last year after my husband left me," she said. "But look at me now. I'm still working and everything is OK."

[Excerpt from Transcript www.cnn.com]
"I'm still working and everything is OK." These were Antoinette's words to the gunman who authorities say they had reason to believe was getting ready to open fire at an elementary school in Atlanta, GA.

Later, I saw an interview where the reporter asked Antoinette what she said to the gunman to try to calm him down:

"I just started telling him my story and how my life turned for me last year and how rough it was for me and how I fell at my low and felt that no one loved me and how I had a multiple disabled child and just lost my husband after 33 years and he was the only man that I knew since I was 13 yrs old and look at me, I'm still living. I explained to him that I just opened up a brand new business, and I'm getting back out there so it's alright... life will bring about turns but we can live... in spite of what it looks like."

[Interview from GAWKER. http://gawker.com/how-one-woman-talked-the-would-be-georgia-school-shoote-1178217739]

Life is a decision. You've got to choose to be happy and make the most out of even the most challenging of circumstances. I make a decision everyday to get better no matter what obstacles come my way. As a matter of fact, my success is indebted to my pain, because I used my pain to push me to Greatness.

You might be thinking, "My boss is crazy; my wife isn't acting right; my kids are out of control; my money isn't right; etc." But none of these things matter when you consider the Big picture. Look at the negative and turn it around - you only get one life, one opportunity, ONE shot!

DAY ONE: LEARN IT

What does it mean to turn lemons into lemonade? Loosely put, there is pleasure and opportunities in even the worst situations.

By her own admission, Antoinette was recently divorced after 33 years of marriage and had a handicapped son but

> ...there is pleasure and opportunities in even the worst

managed to pick up the pieces of her life and start her own business.

She was alone with an unstable gunman and, instead of kicking herself for showing up to work on her day off and sitting in muted fear, she connected with the gunman and shared her own struggles with him and, in turn, not only saved her life, but the lives of several elementary school children, faculty, and staff. There could have been parents mourning over their children for the rest of their lives. But instead, they get to remember the courageous efforts of a woman who was strong enough to rise above her circumstances.

There are hundreds of other examples of people who take hardship and turn it into something they can later celebrate about.

We've talked a little about Michael Jordan earlier, but his resulting victories after not being picked for his high school varsity team, illustrate what can happen when someone eventually gets pleasure from an unfortunate situation.

Lucille Ball, the famous red-head from *I Love Lucy* was told that she couldn't act before she became a hit and starred in one of the most popular TV shows of all times.

Bethany Hamilton, a professional surfer, is known world wide not only for surviving a fatal shark attack that left her without her left arm, but also for overcoming her injuries and returning back to surfing.

In the mid 90's, Apple and Marvel (one of the world's leading comic book brands) were at the bottom of their games. But thanks to persistent efforts and creations, such as the iPhone and the iPad, Apple is once again one of the world's leading brands. And a once bankrupt Marvel, made itself appealing enough to be purchased by Disney.

Any one of these examples can be used to illustrate many of the lessons that we've discussed in this book (i.e., Taking advantage of opportunities, Bringing your "A" game, etc.), but I use them here to emphasize that though upsets are inevitable, so are comebacks if you are willing to put in the work to make it happen.

I dropped out of high school, left home, and was homeless, eating out of garbage cans. But when someone challenged me to do something to make my life better, I had a decision to make - sink or swim.

Back when we were dating, my wife, Dede, said it plain, "Eric, I'm leaving to go to college and I don't want a long distance relationship." I hated school, but I knew that if I remained behind, I would get lost in the streets and, I knew that I would lose my girl. Looking back, I realize that I could have sat in my anger towards my mom for keeping the secret about my real dad, and to some , I may even have been justified, but where would that have gotten me? I couldn't get better by sabotaging myself. Neither can you.

> ...upsets are inevitable but so are comebacks if you are willing to put in the work to make it happen.

In general, how do you handle major upsets or disappointments?

_____

_____

_____

DAY TWO: ACCEPT IT

Think about some of the "lemons" that life has thrown you (i.e., fatherless home, death of a parent/child, laid off from your job, failed company, etc.). How did you handle this situation? What outlets did you use to push you forward? Who were the key people involved in helping you move ahead? Who were the key people involved in keeping you behind?

_____

_____

_____

_____

DAY THREE: EMBRACE IT

Sometimes it's not the hand you're dealt, it's how you play it; you've got to have a poker face. Don't allow one bad moment to turn into a bad day.

Below are 4 cards with 4 different "lemon" scenarios. Underneath each card, write what your initial reaction to the situation would be and then describe a reaction that would allow you to move on with your day in a more healthy way (i.e., make lemonade).

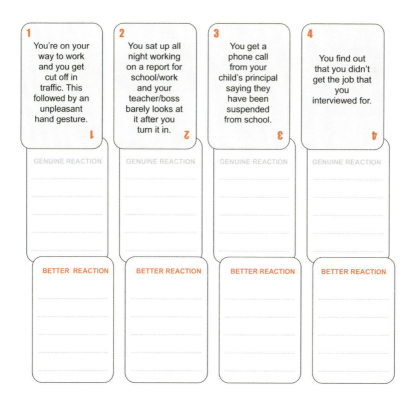

DAY FOUR: CHANGE IT

Our hardships work to make us stronger - if we allow them. It's important to understand the value in optimism and the need for growth. Both of these things will help to position you for Greatness.

Maybe you've already mastered perseverance and making the most out of unfavorable circumstances. But if you haven't, what changes would you need to make to become a person who makes the best out of a bad day, week, month, or year? The steps below helped me to make my transition:

Preparation

Being prepared is number one on this list because I've learned that it's easier to persevere and press through hardships when you understand that they are a natural part of life. You can't always know when disaster is going to hit, but being aware of the possibility puts you in the best position to move past it.

Taking ownership

Most "lemons" we experience are a result of decisions that we've made. This doesn't always mean that the decisions are bad, but it is a fact that decisions come with consequences, and that's ok. Remember, when we don't see our role, we play the "blame game" and open the door to a Victim's Mentality. (If necessary, revisit the chapters on Taking Ownership and Victim's Mentality).

Positive Thinking

Remember, negative thoughts destroy success.

Resilience

The only time a fall is embarrassing is when you refuse to get back up. Keep it moving.

Think about three major set backs in your life and describe how those set backs could work together to create something positive. Or how has it already worked in your favor? Write your answers in your GIUY Success Journal.

_____

_____

DAY FIVE: LIVE IT

What do you need to do to make sure that you're not allowing yourself to get caught up by the obstacles that life throws in your path? How will you personally be able to find the pleasure or make the most out of unfortunate situations? Create your 7-day plan for this area and commit to using it next week.

SUNDAY   *i.e., Write my 7-day plan ...*_____

_____

*Use your GIUY Success Journal to write out your plan.

Greatness Is...

I did some research on Adele a while back and discovered that when she was trying to record the album, 21, that she would spend hours in the studio but, eventually, she had to stop the project for months because the creativity wasn't at the level that it needed to be. But then her man, at the time, broke up with her. And not only did he break up with her, he got with someone else and was engaged in a matter of weeks.

She was talented. She was gifted. She already had her share of successes but after that breakup, she thought that her world had ended; but she didn't just sit in the pain and let it consume her. She was broken, but she didn't let herself stay there. She would have been justified in doing any number of things considering the circumstances, but instead, she got up and went back to the studio and belted out a record breaking album, earning seven Grammys, two Brit awards, twelve Billboard awards, and the list goes on.

In one move, she altered the course of her whole life out of the pain of the thing that she thought would destroy her.

Greatness is refusing to allow yourself to get beat out of the opportunity to fully realize your potential.

Spend time today reflecting on your actions this week.

Did you meet the challenge? If not, why?

_____

_____

_____

_____

SUMMARY OF THE WEEK

THINK ABOUT "LEMONS" LIFE HAS THROWN YOU

How did you handle this situation?

What outlets did you use to push you forward?

Who were the key people involved in helping you move ahead?

Who were the key people involved in keeping you behind?

SOMETIMES IT'S NOT THE HAND YOU'RE DEALT IT'S HOW YOU PLAY IT

YOU'VE GOT TO HAVE A POKER FACE

what changes would you need to make to become a person who makes the best out of a bad day, week, month, or year?

- RESILIENCE
- POSITIVE THINKING
- TAKING OWNERSHIP
- PREPARATION

DESCRIBE HOW THOSE SET BACKS WORKED TOGETHER TO CREATE SOMETHING POSITIVE

THREE MAJOR SETBACKS

GREATNESS IS UPON YOU
CERTIFICATE OF COMPLETION

This is to certify that

_____

has successfully completed this week's challenge.

Eric Thomas and Associates, LLC

_____
signature

_____
date

WEEK

21

WORDS OF GREATNESS

DEVELOP
to bring out the capabilities or possibilities of; to cause to grow or expand

DESERT VS. VISION

When you're looking at a desert, do you see mounds of endless sand or endless opportunities?

When life knocks you down, it's a necessity to know who you are, what you want out of life, and why you want it. In short, nothing should be able to make you break your commitment to your vision. You may have to make adjustments depending on the "lemons" that come your way, but you still must move on with the vision in mind.

WEEK 21

"Believe that one day you are not going to live in the world that was given to you, but in the world that you actually dream of."

Eric Thomas

DEVELOP YOUR DESERT

Last week, we looked at a few examples of people who turned their life around for the better in spite of obstacles, and we took a general look at how you handle setbacks in general, and discussed a few things you can do to change behavior that would keep you from being able to successfully adapt to adversity.

This week, we take a closer look at how you can create new opportunities even when other opportunities have failed.

Many people forget this, but before all the lights, glitter, and glamour, Las Vegas was a desert. All it took was one man with a vision to change the world, he lived in into the world he dreamed of. Most people have sight but few people have vision - you are never at the mercy of the world that was given to you; you can create a better world.

When I travel, people often ask me, "How did you get from being homeless and a high school drop-out to where you are today?" And the answer is always the same, "I had to see something that I was not before I was."

When I was out in the streets, a Pastor came to me and said, "Eric, you have something great in you. You are going to be a leader, a motivator, and a community activist." I didn't believe him at the time because, let's just be honest, he was a Pastor. Pastors always find something good to say about people - its a rite of passage. One encounter with this man changed my life, because he gave me something that no one had ever given me before - a vision.

I told him that what he was saying was impossible, because no one in my family had ever been to college. He looked me in the eyes and said, "That's why they call it history, son. You're going to make history." All of my accomplishments have come from him believing in me before I knew to believe in myself.

Vision. Even though things weren't great in my environment, I developed a mental picture of where I wanted to be and what I wanted to do - I was homeless once and now I have a beautiful home because, even though my circumstances were homelessness, my vision wasn't homelessness.

I don't care where you're from or what your current circumstances are, if you're going to be successful, you have to wake up every single morning with your vision in mind - even in the midst of temporary setbacks. You have the power to develop your desert.

DAY ONE: LEARN IT

My team and I vowed never to bring this up again, but what I'm getting ready to tell you is such a good example of how having a vision and maintaining that vision in the midst of a setback, works to keep you moving toward your goal.

Here's an example of a huge mistake we made that we had to turn into a learning opportunity:

We were really excited about how well my autobiography, *The Secret to Success* was selling and decided that it would be great to do message shirts with our signature catch phrase, "When you want to succeed as bad as you want to breathe..." We got with a graphic designer, he made the design, and we all decided that we loved it. CJ was geeked. I was geeked. The whole squad was excited! We just knew that this was going to be a hit. We started picking out colors, emailing the design to family and friends, telling people to look out for it - everything. CJ placed the order with the shirt company and when they sent us the proof before they went to print, CJ, Karl, LaShanna, and I all saw the proof and said that it was good to go. We even sent the proof over to a few other friends and family just to make sure, and they said the same. We approved of the proof and the shirts went to print. Weeks go by and we finally get the package we had been waiting for. I opened the first box of 50 boxes and pulled out a shirt and there it was as plain as day: WHEN YOU WANT TO SUCCEED AS BAD AS YOU WANT TO B-R-E-A-T-H.

We were dumbfounded. Where was the "E" that was supposed to go at the end of the word B-R-E-A-T-H-E? As it turned out, we accidentally approved the wrong proof. So there we were with 1,000 B-R-E-A-T-H shirts instead of B-R-E-A-T-H-E shirts.

We spent money to get 1,000 shirts that we would never be able to sell. We stood looking at each other devastated. We dwelled in our sorrow for about 30 minutes, and then everybody went back to work. We didn't waste time arguing about who was wrong or right. We looked at how the mistake was made, called the guy back the next day, placed a new order, put systems in place to make sure it didn't happen again and then we got back on our grind; because when you want to succeed as bad as you want to breathe, you don't have time to lose sight of the vision.

A desert can be a missed opportunity or an area in your life where you can't see the potential right away. Take a moment to think about the dessert in your life.

DAY TWO: ACCEPT IT

Developing your desert is not an overnight process. Begin with the end in mind. Yesterday, I told you to start each day with your vision in mind. To be successful at this, you actually need to (1) identify your vision and (2) start your day with that vision in mind.

The Pastor told me that I was going to college and, when I could actually see it for myself, I woke up every morning with that goal in my head. Today, identify your vision and create a Morning Statement. It can be as complicated or as simple as you need it to be. For me, my Morning Statement was: "I am going to college." As time moved on, it changed little by little until a new vision became necessary.

Original Morning Statement:

"I am going to college."

Adapted Morning Statement:

"I am applying to college this fall."

Adapted Morning Statement:

"I am leaving for college next week."

Adapted Morning Statement:

"I am going to get my Master's Degree."

CHALLENGE

Write your Morning Statement below or in your Success Journal. Rewrite it and put it somewhere you can see it every morning.

Original Morning Statement:

DAY THREE: EMBRACE IT

Everyone isn't as fortunate as I was to have had someone to come up to me and give me direction. But you don't need that experience to get the same results. If you had trouble yesterday creating your Morning Statement or if you are having a hard time visualizing in general, try answering the following question: If you were to die today, what would you want to be included in your eulogy? What type of lifestyle do you want to be remembered for living? Who do you hope to have impacted?

DAY FOUR: CHANGE IT

Many of the people who watch my TGIMs write down the principles so that they can come back to them and study them. The principles I speak of were developed from my life's experiences - mistakes that I've made, things that I've learned, and challenges that I had to personally overcome.

Today, create a list of your own Principles to live by.

DAY FIVE: LIVE IT

Remember, you can use your pain to push you to greatness but you'll need a vision. Create your 7-day plan of how you will work to define your vision or steps you will take to make your vision a reality.

SUNDAY   *i.e., Write my 7-day plan ...*
_____

*Use your GIUY Success Journal to write out your plan.

Greatness Is...

In the Bible, there is a story about a man named Jacob who met a woman, who would shortly thereafter, become the love of his life, Rachel. Desperately in love, he went to her father and told him that he would work seven years to have her hand in marriage. Rachel's father agreed that he would rather Rachel marry Jacob than anyone else, and so Jacob began to work. These seven years felt like nothing to Jacob, because he was so in love and so focused on the end goal.

When the seven years were complete, he went to Rachel's father for her hand in marriage. There was a huge wedding, and they became husband and wife... or so Jacob thought. As it turned out, the woman that he married was Leah, Rachel's older sister. When Jacob confronted Rachel's dad about the deception, he explained that it was against their custom to allow the youngest daughter to get married before the eldest. Rachel's father promised Jacob that, if he worked another seven years, he would give him Rachel's hand in marriage. Jacob worked those additional seven years with as much passion and fervor as he did the first seven because in spite of the fact that he was tricked and set back from his original plans, his vision was to marry Rachel, and he was willing to do whatever he needed to do to be with her.

What am I saying? Listen, sometimes things don't work out the way we planned. We can do everything right - dot every "i", cross every "t," but somehow someone or something (some trauma or event) interrupts the flow. Jacob would have had every right to be pissed. He could have walked away with Leah and never returned, he could have left Leah behind altogether and just abort his whole plan, or any number of other things. But instead he chose to make the adjustment with his vision in mind, and he worked the additional seven years to get what he wanted. For fourteen years Jacob got up everyday thinking, "I'm going to marry Rachel." Life without her was his desert, but he knew what he needed to do to change it.

> Greatness is not just about making the best out of whatever life gives you, it's also about commitment to your vision at all costs.

Spend time today reflecting on your actions this week.

Did you meet the challenge? If not, why?

SUMMARY OF THE WEEK

TO BE SUCCESSFUL

(1) identify your vision
(2) start your day with that vision in mind.

What would you want to be included in your eulogy?

What type of lifestyle do you want to be remembered for living?

Who do you hope to have impacted?

CREATE YOUR MORNING STATEMENT

CREATE A LIST OF YOUR OWN
PRINCIPLES TO LIVE BY

GREATNESS IS UPON YOU
CERTIFICATE OF COMPLETION

This is to certify that

_____

has successfully completed this week's challenge.

Eric Thomas and Associates, LLC

_____
signature

_____
date

WEEK

22

WORDS OF GREATNESS

PERFORM
to carry out; do

PERFORM VS. OUTPERFORM

Are you content with the success you've acquired at this point or are you ready for the next challenge?

You can perform and stay in the pocket, or you can push yourself to the next level and set the standard there as well. In this chapter we look at different performance levels and discuss why it's important to move out of the pocket.

WEEK 22

"You don't get what you want out of life. You get what you've earned."

Eric Thomas

OUTPERFORM YOURSELF

So what if you're already the CEO of your company? What if you already have your dream job and doing all the things you've hoped to accomplish by this time in your life? What do you do when you're already on top? When you've reached the point in your life where you have bested the best, don't get comfortable. Don't become complacent. Step back into the ring and outperform yourself.

DAY ONE: LEARN IT

Repeat this statement: I am where I am today because of what I did yesterday. But what I did yesterday is not going to help me tomorrow.

"One hit wonder" is a term frequently used in the music industry to describe a singer or artist who only had one hit or signature song. However, this term is applicable to anyone with a single success. You are only as good as your last hit. This is why there is never any time for complacency.

I didn't just stop at speaking in schools. I pushed myself to speak to athletic teams and then major corporations. I watch my own videos and take notes to see how I can improve on my next opportunity. Even still, I didn't limit myself to just speaking. I started my own Consulting Firm, Eric Thomas and Associates, LLC and brought in people who grind just as hard as I do to help build the company. We do consulting in education, athletics, and executive coaching, and we even have a store where you can purchase inspirational material (i.e., books, shirts, dvds, etc.). Every venture may not be an immediate hit, but I've created opportunities within my opportunities to set more records.

 As most of you know, my rise to public visibility stemmed from the success of the *Secret to Success* speech (The Guru Story). I remember when the video first went viral and it started to reach views in the millions. My team and I were in awe! We watched as the views continued to climb higher and higher. Everywhere I went people would stop me and ask, "Are you the guy from the Guru" story?

At first I didn't see a problem with it. I mean, the brand was finally starting to gain momentum and we were being recognized for putting out a great product. Then I began to worry. I remember thinking to myself, "I have more to offer than just that story. Are people going to see me as a one hit wonder?" I even stopped doing the Guru story for a period of time so that people would know I had more in my arsenal. My *Thank God It's Monday* YouTube series was gaining steam, but still nothing like the "Guru Story". So my team and I went back to the lab to produce more content in the same vein as that story.

Next thing you knew, we had tons of videos going viral! It seemed like every month there was a new video taking off!

From, *Whats your Why* to *Greatness Is Upon You*, people were starting to see that I had more to offer than that one video. So while I am utterly grateful for the success of the *Guru Story* video and love everything it represents, I understood that if we didn't get busy quick, people would move on to the next phenomenon.

If you don't want to be a one hit wonder, you have to keep grinding. You can't trophy watch and get so caught up in your accomplishments that you're looking at the score board instead of playing the game. You cannot settle.

What is your latest success?

DAY TWO: ACCEPT IT

Kobe said that the thing that drives him is his desire to be the best. He has an assassin's mentality. He knows the reason he gets up every morning. He understands his purpose. He doesn't just show up to the game...he becomes the game.

Shade in your level of performance in each of the areas above. Be honest with yourself. You will see that you might be a Peak performer in one area and only a level performer in other areas.

- **Level Performers** - Do what is minimally required. They show up to work, school, or their kid's music recital, but there is no additional investment of time, energy, or effort.
- **Peak Performers** - Do what is required and will do more if pushed or asked by someone in authority or by a loved one.

- **Elite Performers** - Do more than what is required and are happy to do so. They move independent of coaxing and put in extra time, energy, and effort.

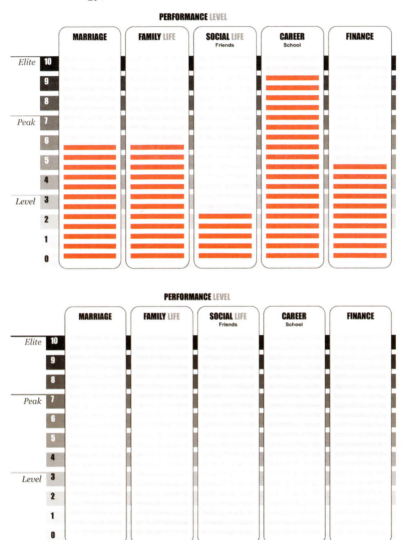

DAY THREE: EMBRACE IT

Find one person who you trust from each of the areas in Day Two and ask them to rate what level of performance they think you are on in the area that is relevant to them. For example, you would ask your husband, wife, or significant other to shade in your level of performance in the "Marriage/Romantic Relationship" section. At the end of the day, compare your answers from Day Two with the ones you received today. What are the consistencies? Inconsistencies?

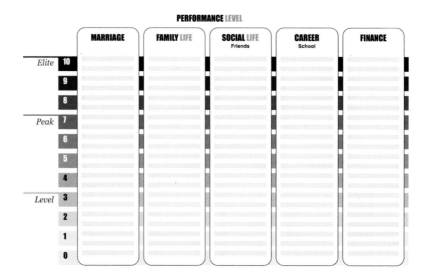

DAY FOUR: CHANGE IT

Today, plan the process. What are you going to do to make it from Peak Performance to Elite Performance in your Peak Performing areas? What are you going to do to move from Level to Peak Performance? How can moving from one level to the next help you in that specific area in the long term? Who stands to benefit from you going to the next level?

DAY FIVE: LIVE IT

Question: If a car operates at 6 gears, why would you only drive it on 4? You're wasting potential. Everyone has the potential to be better. Make a move today to move to the next level of performance in two areas of your life (i.e., financially, in your career, in school, etc.). What are you prepared to commit to doing differently that you have not done this year? Create your 7-day plan.

SUNDAY *i.e., Write my 7-day plan ...*

*Use your GIUY Success Journal to write out your plan.

GREATNESS IS...

Oprah Winfrey is arguably one of the most influential people on the planet. She is one of the best examples of outperforming yourself in the public eye today. Most people know her from her history making talk show, The Oprah Winfrey Show, *which was the highest rated program of its time. No one would have blamed her for staying in the pocket and limiting her career to being a phenomenal talk show host, but she didn't stop there. She is CEO of Harpo Productions, CEO of the Oprah Winfrey Network, she founded the Oprah Winfrey Academy for Girls in South Africa, and the list goes on.*

If you're already where you want to be in life, that's great, but what's next on the agenda? The potential for success is like a muscle, you have to exercise it if you want to take full advantage of it. If you stop working the muscle, your ability to sustain your status diminishes, and you become a "One Hit Wonder."

Greatness is expanding your portfolio to create more opportunities to stretc.h yourself.

Spend time today reflecting on your actions this week.

Did you meet the challenge? If not, why?

_____

_____

_____

_____

_____

SUMMARY OF THE WEEK

IF YOU DON'T WANT TO BE A ONE HIT WONDER

SET MORE RECORDS

LEVEL PERFORMERS
Do what is minimally required. They show up to work, school, or their kid's music recital but there is no additional investment of time, energy, or effort.

ELITE PERFORMERS
Do more than what is required and are happy to do so. They move independent of coaxing and put in extra time, energy, and effort.

PEAK PERFORMERS
Do what is required and will do more if pushed or asked by someone in authority or by a loved one.

P E L

YOU CAN BE A PEAK PERFORMER IN ONE AREA AND ONLY A LEVEL PERFORMER IN OTHER AREAS.

Find one person who you trust, ask them to rate what

LEVEL OF PERFORMANCE
THEY THINK YOU ARE ON

GREATNESS IS UPON YOU
CERTIFICATE OF COMPLETION

This is to certify that

_____

has successfully completed this week's challenge.

Eric Thomas and Associates, LLC

_____
signature

_____
date

WEEK 23

WORDS OF GREATNESS

RESILIENT
springing back; recovering readily from illness, depression, adversity, or the like

KNOCKED DOWN VS. BOUNCE BACK

When you get hit, are you down for the count or are you back on your feet?

In previous chapters we discussed creating more opportunities out of misfortune and the importance of committing to your vision. The glue that makes either of these things possible is resilience.

WEEK 23

"I used the pain to push me to Greatness."

Eric Thomas

PHENOMENAL

GREAT

GOOD

AVERAGE

BOUNCE BACK

"Professor Choudhry, I would like to make an appointment with you during your office hours to discuss how I can improve my grade in your class. I know I failed my first exam, but I was hoping that if I started early, you could work with me on some extra problems," LaShanna said, hopeful that her Calculus professor would see her enthusiasm and eagerness to improve.

"Ms. Fountain," Professor Choudhry said as he walked around his desk, "you made a score of 15 out of a possible 100 points. There is absolutely no way you will pass my class. I don't give extra credit, and the scores that you would have to make in order to even come close are obviously outside of your capabilities. It would be better for you to drop the course now and save yourself the trouble."

 She told this story to the team one morning during a staff meeting in a discussion about fighting the odds. She left her professor's classroom that day devastated by her professor's comments, but she got up the next morning determined to come out of that Calculus class with a passing grade. Everyday for the next three and half months, she did practice exam after practice exam, she spent two hours a day in the math lab, she sat in the front of the class, she cut her party life down tremendously , she sacrificed "the college life", and she looked her Professor in the eyes every class and asked questions. At the end of each class, she would walk past her Professor, look him square in the eyes, and say, "Thank you, Professor Choudhry, I appreciate your time. I'll see you next class."

She scored at least a 90% on each exam after her first failed exam, a 95% on the final, and walked away with an 89% in a class that her Professor told her to drop because she would never pass.

DAY ONE: LEARN IT

Everyone is capable of success, but most people fail because they aren't able to recover from setbacks. They quit because someone told them that they couldn't do it. They stop because they didn't get the results they expected. They shift gears when it gets too hard.

> Everyone is capable of success, but most people fail because they aren't able to recover from setbacks.

I believe that people deal with setbacks in one of three ways:

They fall and never recover, refusing to try again.

People in this category get hit by devastations (i.e., lost loved ones, financial upsets, missed opportunities, failed attempts at meeting goals, etc.) and completely give up. Imagine throwing a rubber ball at a wall and watching it fall directly to the floor - immobile. They allow themselves to be overcome by negative thinking and almost always have a Victim's Mentality. They say things like, "This never works out for me so I quit," "There's no point in trying," "Everyone gets ahead except me." They are the type of people who would get a 15 on an exam and not only drop the class from fear of failing again but possibly never set foot in that class or any other advanced math course again.

They fall and instead of staying focused on their goal, they get distracted by their failure(s) and shift gears, abandoning the original goal.

People who fall in this category are never able to reach their full potential, because they prematurely jump ship and end up moving in a multitude of different directions. I find that people in this category often confuse bouncing back with merely bouncing. It would be the difference between throwing a rubber ball against a wall and having it come directly back to you and throwing a rubber ball, and it ricochets in a million different directions. They often change course with every bad turn of events. They are the type of people who would get a 15 on an exam and decide that any degree where math is a requirement for them is not an option and change to a major where the courses aren't as challenging. For them, it's not a matter of them thinking that things never work out for them as in the first group, but more a matter of them shifting gears before exhausting every possible option; as a result, they end up moving around in circles, never fulfilling a goal, because every time they get hit, they never fully bounce back but, instead, they bounce around.

They fall and get back up, exhausting every possible opportunity for meeting their goal before they make a decision that would be better suited for them.

The fact is, sometimes, you have to make adjustments to your course. Everyone won't die a Grammy winning artist. Everyone can't make the NBA draft. Everyone can't be a CEO of a Fortune 500 company. Resilient people experience upsets differently than the other two groups. They get knocked down, and they get up and try again. They keep trying, exhausting every possibility before altering their course.

I told you, it took me twelve years to get a four-year degree. There were so many times when I wanted to throw in the towel completely and just be content with where I was. There were even more times when I thought about changing my course and pursuing other goals but, ultimately, I knew that with every failed attempt, I learned something that I didn't know before; that new knowledge eventually created the platform for my success. So no matter how many times I failed, I couldn't give up; if there was an avenue, a method, or any means left unexplored to help me meet my goals, I got up and I took it.

Which category do you fit into?

DAY TWO: ACCEPT IT

Complete the following statements:

CHALLENGE

When dealing with setbacks, I habitually do the following

_____

_____

_____

This usually results in

_____

_____

_____

I have (not) been able to meet the following goals due to how I handled the situation

_____

_____

_____

DAY THREE: EMBRACE IT

Create a scenario unique to your life where you are hit with disappointments from multiple directions. Forecast what systems or strategies you would put in place to help you to bounce back on your feet.

DAY FOUR: CHANGE IT

If you have trouble with being resilient, it's never too late in the game to make a change. Many of the lessons we've discussed up to this point are useful in helping you to become more able to adapt to changes in your environment. Visit or revisit the ones that are applicable to your needs:

- Positive Thinking vs. Negative Thinking
- Victim vs. Victor
- Turning Lemons into Lemonade
- Developing your Desert

DAY FIVE: LIVE IT

Don't miss out on anymore opportunities. Create a 7-day plan that will help you to build your resiliency.

SUNDAY   *i.e., Write my 7-day plan ...*
_____

_____

*Use your GIUY Success Journal to write out your plan.

Greatness Is...

In 1928, Walt Disney experienced a setback so major that he thought his whole career was on the decline. He made the mistake of signing away the ownership rights to his first successful cartoon to a New York distributor and had to walk away with practically nothing. But this didn't stop him. After getting burned, Walt vowed never to work for anyone else ever again. Walt knew that in order to save his studio, he had to come up with a new character and so was birthed Mickey Mouse and, shortly after, Disneyland.

He learned from his mistake, became knowledgable in intellectual property, continued to work on his craft and now, Walt Disney is a household name. And he was able to accomplish all of this because he never stopped trying.

I told you before, you can't just kind of want it. Sometimes to get back up and keep fighting you have to reach beyond yourself and remember why you set out to do the thing you started to begin with. If you're going to be Great, you've got to have stamina. The race isn't given to the strong, it's given to the ones who can endure.

The problem with many of us, the reason we can't bounce back, is because we lack endurance. We get hit and we stay down, because it's easier to avoid a challenge than it is to stand up to it. We want to compete with the Greats, but we don't even have the courage to get in the ring.

Let me tell you something, an oak tree is just a nut that held it's ground. You don't always have to be smarter, stronger, or faster than the next guy; some fights, you just have to want it enough to stay in the ring.

Greatness is having the fortitude to get up after being knocked down.

Spend time today reflecting on your actions this week.

Did you meet the challenge? If not, why?

GREATNESS IS UPON YOU
CERTIFICATE OF COMPLETION

This is to certify that

_____

has successfully completed this week's challenge.

Eric Thomas and Associates, LLC

_____
signature

_____
date

WEEK

24

WORDS OF GREATNESS

APPLICATION
the act of putting to a special use or purpose

WASTED INFORMATION VS. APPLICATION

Are you wasting information or are you applying it appropriately?

The first step is getting the information. The hard step is applying it. This week we discuss the importance of applying information to your life so that you can begin to see the results you sought the information out for to begin with.

WEEK 24

"Man's greatness consists in his ability to do and the proper application of his powers to the things needed to be done."

Frederick Douglas

APPLY, THEN PUSH !

When I was a kid, my mother and I would go to the grocery store every Saturday morning. I used to love going with her because, after we would leave the check-out, I would always stop by the gumball machines. There was a prize machine there that contained temporary tattoos. My mom and I had a deal; if I behaved while shopping, she would give me a quarter, and I could get a temporary tattoo.

When I first started getting the tattoos, I would become disappointed because the tattoo would wear off after 30 minutes; hardly even enough time to show my friends. One particular day, my mother watched as I applied my tattoo and quickly pointed out the fact that I was doing it wrong.

For one, I was putting too much water on the tattoo. Two, I was not applying enough pressure. Sure enough, she was right. From that day forward, I used her method to apply the tattoo and found much greater success and longevity.

Once you gather the needed information, it is critical to understand the importance of applying it correctly. There was nothing wrong with the tattoos I bought; the problem was that I was not applying them the way they were meant to be applied.

DAY ONE: LEARN IT

As with everything, application is key! As humans, everyday we go in search of new information, hoping that, once we find it, it magically improves our lives. Whether it be buying that new book, registering for that new class, or aimlessly searching the web, we all search for new information everyday.

As a general rule, seeking out lots of information is great. However, the problem begins when we start preferring quantity over quality. We load our brains with tons of information but often times forget the most critical part, applying it!

Think of what your life would look like if you literally applied all the things you've read in self-help books. Where would you be physically if you implemented all the exercise and diet techniques you read about in the health and wellness magazines?

The point I am trying to make is that information is everywhere, and gaining as much of it as possible should be your goal. But if I had to choose between a person who learned 10 things and applied 8 vs. the person who learned 500 things and only applied 2, guess who I want on my team.

I'll never forget being at a presentation and telling students that "Knowledge is Power", but then my mentee, Walt, pulled me to the side and said, "E, knowledge itself isn't necessarily power. Applied knowledge is power."

I wrote this book in a manual style format because it is my belief that any and everyone has what it takes to be successful if provided the correct information. But getting the information is only step 1. Steps 2-100 involve applying it!

How many opportunities have you missed out on because you failed to apply your knowledge on the subject?

DAY TWO: ACCEPT IT

Remember, there is a difference between the things that you have learned and those things that you have successfully been able to apply to your life. Consider the chapters in this book that were most applicable to your life. In the space below or in your GIUY Success Journal, indicate what lessons you learned; in the space next to it, note whether you have successfully applied those lessons to your life.

_____

_____

_____

_____

DAY THREE: EMBRACE IT

In my tattoo story, I told you that my mom said that I wasn't applying enough pressure to my tattoos and, as a result, they weren't lasting as long as they should have. Similarly, many of you have yet to see the results you desire out of life because you get the information and you may even use it for a while, but you aren't pushing yourself to that next level.

What extra steps can you take today to add the necessary pressure you need to realize your full potential? For example, maybe you need to recommit yourself to your purpose, or maybe you need to spend extra time in a few of the chapters in this book until the lessons become second nature.

DAY FOUR: CHANGE IT

Change can begin as early as today. Before diving head first into a project or opportunity, stop and ask yourself...

- Do I have the information I need to get started?
- Do I know the correct way in which to apply the information?
- Am I willing to deal with the pressure associated with the task?
- What can I do to push myself to be consistent and demand change?

Over the last few years, I have watched my team and I go from information gatherers to information producers. It's been remarkable to watch the changes that occur when information is applied.

I've always been told that teaching someone what you've learned is the best way to retain information, and I've further learned that it's an awesome tool for accountability.

I share new information with my team everyday, and they hold me accountable.

What lessons or information from this book can you share with someone you know?

_____

_____

_____

_____

DAY FIVE: LIVE IT

Now that you have the information, what plan will you put in gear to apply the information to your own life?

SUNDAY   *i.e., Write my 7-day plan ...*
_____

_____

*Use your GIUY Success Journal to write out your plan.

GREATNESS IS...

You can be Great.

I started studying the Greats, and what I realize about the Greats is that it's not about talent. The difference between the Good and the Great is about Mentality - it's all or nothing. What you did last week doesn't count, you are as current as the present moment, you have to play every single play as if it were your last. And you have to play it with the mindset of a Champion - "I can. I Will. I MUST."

The Greats didn't necessarily wake up every morning thinking, "Today, I'm going to be Great." But the thing that separates them from everyone else is that they got up every day and did the ordinary extraordinarily.

Greatness isn't something that happens over night. It's an ongoing process that starts with waking up everyday and taking full advantage of the time and opportunities that have been gifted to you.

I get out of bed every morning at 3 am, and I pour 120% into every opportunity that God has given me. Because when I go out to speak, my son is depending on me, my daughter is depending on me... my wife and mom are depending on me... my company depends on me. There are children all over the country who watch me and say, "... if ET can be a high school dropout and take 12 years to get a 4-year degree and now be only weeks away from getting his PhD, then I've got a chance..."

I don't get to let them down. My excuses won't provide them with what they need. I've got an opportunity of a lifetime, and I've got to take advantage of it.

When we began, I told you that this book was an opportunity for you to rewrite your history. It doesn't matter if you've failed to meet your goals. It doesn't matter that you've endured disappointment after disappointment. It doesn't matter that you're not where life says you should be at this stage in your life. And it doesn't matter how selfish, self-centered, or self-involved you were in your past, or how many opportunities you've missed or waited too long for. All that matters is the answer to this question today: Now that you have information that could change your life, what are you going to do about it? Are you going to take advantage of it? Or will you let it sit and collect dust?

Greatness is upon you.

Spend time today reflecting on your actions this week.

Did you meet the challenge? If not, why?

SUMMARY OF THE WEEK

Getting the information is only
STEP 1

STEP 2-100
… involves applying it!

EXTRA STEPS

What extra steps can you take today to add the necessary pressure you need to realize your full potential?

BEFORE DIVING HEAD FIRST
into a project or opportunity, stop and ask yourself …

Do I have the information I need to get started?

Do I know the correct way in which to apply the information?

Am I willing to deal with the pressure associated with the task?

What can I do to push myself to be consistent and demand change?

WHAT LESSONS OR INFORMATION FROM THIS BOOK CAN YOU SHARE WITH SOMEONE YOU KNOW?

GREATNESS IS UPON YOU
CERTIFICATE OF COMPLETION

This is to certify that

_____

has successfully completed this week's challenge.

Eric Thomas and Associates, LLC

_____
signature

_____
date

NOTES AND REFERENCES

Some of the material referenced in this book can be found below. As a speaker, especially a speaker who strives to inspire varying platforms, I get the opportunity to share stories in a way that I hope will encourage, uplift, and motivate the masses.

WEEK ONE: REPUTATION VS. CHARACTER

pg.16   Reputations need a light source: *Holt Science and Technology*, Holt, Rinehart, and Winston

WEEK TWO: GETTING CAUGHT VS. CONFESSING

pg. 46   Son of a Monarch who was instructed: 2 Samuel, Holy Bible

WEEK THREE: VICTIM VS. VICTOR

pg.48   Bubonic "Black" Plague: www.science.nationalgeographic.com

WEEK FOUR: NEGATIVE THINKING VS. POSITIVE THINKING

pg. 80   Either make the tree sound: Matthew 12:33, Amplified Bible

WEEK FIVE: GRASSHOPPER VS. THE ANT

pg. 91   Lebron James was put in this position: Howard Beck and Jonathan Abrams, "NBA's Season of pg.91   Suspense Ends," *New York Times*, July, 8th, 2010

pg.91   Merrill Lynch took his shot: Daniel Gross, *Forbes Greatest Business Stories of All Time*, (Byron Preiss Visual Publications, Inc., and Forbes Inc.1996)

pg.91   Curtis Jackson, aka 50 Cent: Dan Charnas, "How 50 Cent scored a half-billion," *The Washington Post*, Sunday, December 19th, 2010

pg.98   Grasshopper and the Ant: Aesop's Fables, www.aesopfables.com

WEEK SIX: MINIMIZE VS. OPTIMIZE

pg.114   Candy Crush Saga: Brendan Sinclair, Candy Crush's recipe for success, GameIndustry International, Nov. 13, 2013

WEEK SEVEN: UNDER THE COMPETITION VS. COMPETITIVE EDGE

pg.122   Muhammad Ali quote: "Rumble in the Jungle" Interview, YouTube

WEEK EIGHT: LEGACY VS. CURRENCY

pg.138   For more information on the Bill Gates Millennium Scholarship, visit www.gmsp.org

WEEK NINE: ALL ABOUT ME VS. RECIPROCITY

pg.160   You can find the parable about the good Samaritan in Luke 10:30-37

WEEK TEN: I GOT TO VS. I GET TO

pgs176-177   A little girl during the depression: This story was influenced by an email that someone sent me years ago along with some fundamental Biblical principals that I adhere to. The recorded version of this story is available on *The Heart of Detroit,* mixtape, which can be downloaded from www.etinspires.com .

WEEK THIRTEEN: THE JUNGLE EXPERIENCE

pg. 228   Sampson and Dellilah: Judges 16

WEEK FOURTEEN: SINK OR SWIM

pg. 242   a Guru and a young man: this is my interpretation of the "Guru" story as seen on YouTube's "Eric Thomas-Secret to Success" video. A friend of mine from college read a section out of the book, *Think and Grow Rich: A Black Choice* by Dennis Kimbro about this guru and a young man. This YouTube video was a major launching pad for my career.

WEEK FIFTEEN: REPEL VS. ATTRACT

pg. 254   Michael Jordan quote: Excerpt from Michael Jordan's Hall of Fame Enshrinement Speech.

WEEK SEVENTEEN: EXTINGUISHING THE FIRE VS. FUELING THE FIRE

pg. 288   The Rabbit and the Turtle: Aesop's Fables, www.aesopfables.com

WEEK EIGHTEEN:

pg.304   Story of Job: Book of Job

WEEK NINETEEN: TAPPED OUT AT 80% VS. ALL IN

pg. 320   Illustration of two men digging for diamonds: Many motivational speakers use this illustration to encourage people not to quit. You can find it in several places online, one of which is www.themetapicture.com/dont-give-up I also use this illustration in my YouTube video, "I CAN, I WILL, I MUST."

WEEK TWENTY: BEATEN VS. BESTED

pg. 328-329 Antoinette Tuff talking down the gunman: This is an incredible story. I found the transcript and an interview at www.cnn.com and www.gawker.com .

pg. 330   Bethany Hamilton: For more on this inspirational story, visit www.bethanyhamilton.com .

pg. 331   Apple and Marvel: www.forbes.com.

WEEK TWENTY-ONE: DESERT VS. VISION

pg.350   a man named Jacob: Genesis 29

WEEK TWENTY-THREE: KNOCKED DOWN VS. BOUNCE BACK

pg. 378   Walt Disney: Daniel Gross, *Forbes Greatest Business Stories of All Time* , *(Byron Preiss Visual Publications, Inc., and Forbes Inc.1996)*

ACKNOWLEDGEMENT

I am truly humbled by every encounter, every conversation, every handshake, every hug, every "Like", every "View", every encouraging word... it all means so much to me.

Thank you to Bob Proctor, Tony Nuckolls, Bill Emerson, Thomas Davis, New Balance Athletic Shoes Inc., Under Armour Inc., Cairo, Egypt, Reggie Bush, Tyrese Gibson, Glenn Twiddle, Incipio Academy, Stephen Tulloch, BK Boreyko, Sean "Diddy" Combs, Omarion, Kaleb ThornhillBrian Bostick, BJ Stabler, June Archer and ESPN, NBC, Anthony "Showtime" Pettis, Duke Rufus, Prince & Chanelle Fielder, Lawrence Frank, Marc Jackson, Geoffrey Smchidt, Niya Butts, Mark Dantonio, Mike Davis, Disclosure, Mikestro, Quicken Loans, Ashley Iserhoff, Tom Izzo, Buffini & Company, Quicken Loans, Kyani, Shaun Harris with AT&T Terry, and all of the other PHENOMENAL people and organizations that I have met over the last few years that have invested in me and given me an opportunity to do what I love.

Oakwood legends who inspired me:
Dennis Ross III, Virtue (mad love for the Trotter sisters) and Shavon Floyd, Sharon Riley and Faith Chorale, Charles Arrington, Angelic Clay, Angela Brown, Brian McKnight, W.S.B. (Willing Succeeding and Black) DP (Owen Simmons), Voice of Triumph (Damien Chandler), Whitney Phips, Barry Black, Chris Willis, Take 6, Dajuan Starling, Paul and Pattrick Graham ("The Twins"), Bell Tower Ministries, Irvin Daphnis, Melvin Hayden, and Connect Five.

Ladies of my life:
Grandma Gwen, Grandma Lama, Auntie Wanda, Auntie Cleo, Auntie Booby, Auntie Tawana for your continued support since diapers. Sister Lamb, Ma Trotter and Ma Bez (Sterline Foster)

Men of my life:
Unlce Bruce, Uncle Jimmy, Tim and Wayne Smith, Robert King, Leon Burnette, Pastor James Doggette, T. Marshall Kelly, Preston Turner, Rupert Cannonier, Jerald Clift Kyle, Renee Chandler, Steve, Pastor James Black, Elder Ward and E. E. Cleveland

Accountability Brothers:
LaDon Daniels, Lee Lamb, Lloyd Paul (S/O St. Marteen), Carlas Quinney, Burks Hollands, Charles Arrington Shannon Austin, Greg Arneaud, Adrian Marsh, John Samon Derrick Green, Quest Green, Joey Kibble, and Karl Phillips.

Thank you to all of my support systems, I couldn't possibly name everyone, but among the many, The Quinney Family, The Tyus Family, The Arrington Family, Walter Bivens and The Advantage Family, A Place of Change Ministries, Rodney Patterson, Murray Edwards, Dr. June, Dr. Curry, Dr. Gunnings, Dr. Dagbovie, Bostick, LBJ, Meek Mill, The Lamb Family, Tobe, Lamar Higgins, Dorthy L. Green, The Austin Family Derek Bowe, and all those mentioned and acknowledged in *The Secret to Success* - I appreciate all of you.

Gone but not forgotten: Uncle Mike, Allen Johnson, Dilsey Moseley Kay Craig-Harper, Renee Braxton, Tawana Braxton-Parker, Renia Braxton, Glenda Craig-Anderson, and MaBez.

Thank you mom and the rest of my family for believing in me.

The ETA Squad (CJ, Karl, LaShanna, Jamal, Kam, Te, Rhondell, Kale, Ken, Mom, and Morgan): I really believe that I have the most talented team in the business and I'm excited about where we're headed.

Thank you to all of the YouTube and Twitter supporters and everyone who has ever purchased a book, wore a T-shirt, downloaded the mixtape, forwarded a video, and the list goes on. Because of you, I get to wake up every morning and do what I was created to do.

To my wife, Dilsey "Dede" Moseley, thank you for being my best friend, my rock, my unyielding accountability partner. You push me to be the best, and that makes me want to give you the best. You, Jalin, and Jayda are my privilege - it doesn't get any better.

Last and always, I give honor to God who shows me everyday that impossible is nothing...

And special thanks to my haters for pushing me to Greatness. Continued blessings on you and your family from hence forth and forever more. *Matthew 5:44*

Grateful,

ET

THANKS FROM THE SQUAD

CARLAS QUINNEY, PRESIDENT

I would like to start by thanking my Mother (Helene) and Father (Carlas). Thank you for being the best parents anyone could ever ask for. To My brothers (Nick and Aaron Quinney), thanks for holding me down from day one! Q Boys for life! To my beautiful wife, thanks for completing me. You are amazing and I thank God everyday for bringing you into my life. To my son Trey, I promise to work as hard as I can to provide for you and your Mom. You two are my why! I love you!

KARL PHILLIPS, MEDIA AND FILM DIRECTOR

I would first like to thank God for simply blessing me with the opportunity to experience this amazing opportunity we know as life! He has surrounded me with a script and cast that make me look like an Oscar worthy actor! To my parents, Walton & Karlene Phillips, I only now understand the advantage I have in life because of your continued commitment to sacrifice of yourselves for my well-being. To my brothers Glenn Phillips & Barry Forde, thank you for guiding me through those tough adolescent years and (Glenn) letting me know who I should date...Which brings me to the person who taught me what love is, my wife Tamesha, I love you with all my heart and thank you for being consistent... Lastly to my first born son Jordan, you truly are a miracle and I promise to do everything in my power to position you for a legacy of Greatness!

LASHANNA FOUNTAIN, DIRECTOR OF OPERATIONS

I was successful because you believed in me.
-Ulysses S. Grant

It's easier to have faith in yourself when you know that the people in your corner have faith in you. I praise God for my corner. They pray and push me to be better and that's more than what most people have - I am rich.

Thank you Eric for not giving up on me and for hanging on to the towel even when others begged you to let it go. I get to work with "ET the Hiphop Preacher" that's my reality when many others can only dream of it.

Thank you Sis Jackson, Ms. Eddrena, Florise Neville-Ewell, and Anneeshia Freeman. It doesn't always turn out the way you think, but somehow you gain in the end. To my brothers Malcolm (my heart), CJ, and Karl, you guys are awesome! Thank you Ashante Tucker and the other ladies of the Diva Mansion, Crystal and Grant, Kamil, Jason, Chinua, Cameo, Serena, and Thay I love you guys. Thank you Healthy 10 Fitness for helping me on my weight loss journey - we're getting it in. To my grandparents, parents, and sisters Michelle and Dana, thank you for believing in me. I appreciate you APOC and Liveoak. I wish I could have you both 24/7. I have so much love for my ETA family, you guys are an inspiration on steroids.

I'm honored, humbled, and committed to the journey...

Best,

-L

WORDS OF GREATNESS

A

Adjustment (ad-just-ment) a modification, fluctuation, or correction.

All (all) the whole of; the greatest possible

Application (app-li-ca-tion) the act of putting to a special use or purpose

Attract (at-trac-t) to draw by appealing to the emotions or sense by stimulating interest or by exciting admiration

C

Championship (cham-pi-on-ship) a contest held to determine a champion

Character (char-ac-ter) the combination of traits and qualities distinguishing the individual nature of a person or thing

Competition (com-pe-ti-tion) the effort of two or more parties acting independently to secure the business of a third party by offering the most favorable terms

Contract (con-tract) a binding agreement between two or more parties; written document

Covenant (cov-e-nant) a binding agreement;

Create (cre-ate) to cause to come into being, as something unique that would not naturally evolve or that is not made by ordinary processes

Currency (cur-ren-cy) money in any form when in actual use; general acceptance

D

Desert (des-ert) an area of water apparently devoid of life

Develop (de-vel-ope) to bring out the capabilities or possibilities of, to cause to grow or expand

Drive (drive) to set or keep in motion or operation

E

Elite (e-lite) the choice or best of anything considered collectively, as of a group or class of persons.

Entitlement (en-tit-le-ment) to give (a person or thing) a title or claim to something

Environment (en-vi-ron-ment) the circumstances, objects, or conditions, by which one is surrounded

Execute (ex-e-cute) To perform or carry out what is required

Expose (ex-pose) to uncover to bare to the air

Extinguish (ex-ting-uish) to put an end to or bring to an end

F

Fuel (fu-el) something that gives nourishment

G

Guru (gu-ru) an intellectual guide or leader

H

Hunt (hunt) to chase or search for; seek; endeavor to obtain or find

I

Investment (in-vest-ment) A commitment as of time or support

J

Jungle (jun-gle) something made up of many confused elements; a bewildering complex or maze

L

Legacy (legacy) something handed down or received from an ancestor or predecessor

Level (lev-el) having no part higher than another; having a flat or even surface.

Leverage (lev-er-age) to improve or enhance; power to accomplish something; strategic advantage.

Lurk (lurk) to lie or wait in concealment; remain in or around a place

M

Meditation (med-i-ta-tion) to engage in thought or contemplation; reflect

O

Ownership (own-ner-ship) the state or fact being the owner or professor of a thing

P

Peak (peak) the maximum point, degree, or volume of anything:

Perform (per-form) to carry out; do

Persevere (per-se-vere) to maintain a purpose in spite of difficulty, obstacles, or discouragement

Perspective (per-spec-tive) subjective evaluation of relative significance; a point of view:

Prestige (pres-tige) reputation or influence arising from success, achievement, rank, or other favorable attributes

Prey (prey) an animal hunted or caught for food

Priority (pri-or-i-ty) something afforded or deserving prior attention

Purpose (pur-pose) the object to which one strives or to which one exists

R

Reciprocity (rec-i-proc-i-ty) a mutual exchange of privileges

Resilient (re·sil·ient) an ability to recover from or adjust easily to misfortune or change

Result (re-sult) the consequence of a particular action, operation, or course

Reputation (rep·u·ta·tion) a specific trait ascribed to a person or thing

Robust (ro-bust) having or exhibiting strength or vigorous health

S

Service (ser-vice) an act of helpful activity

Source (source) the point of origin; One that causes, creates, or initiates; One, such as a person or document, that supplies information

Standard (stan-dard) something, such as a practice or a product, that is widely recognized or employed, especially because of its excellence

T

Thought (thou-ght) the ideas or arrangement of ideas that result from thinking

V

Victim (vic-tim) one that is injured, destroyed, or sacrificed under any of various conditions

Victor (vic-tor) the winner in a fight, battle, contest, or struggle

The Secret To Success

- Hardcover
- eBook
- Audiobook

When you want to succeed as bad as you want to breathe...®

shop.ETinspires.com   Eric Thomas & Associates, LLC.   866.526.3978

[Excerpt from the Award Winning Autobiography, *The Secret to Success*]

Chapter 1

Boiling Point

Anger is a wind which blows out the lamp of the mind. <u>Robert Green Ingersoll</u>

I HATE YOU! I WISH I COULD TAKE BACK THE WORDS I SAID TO HER THAT DAY, BUT I COULDN'T. I SWEAR IT WAS NOT PREMEDITATED. IF I COULD ONLY TURN BACK THE HANDS OF TIME, I WOULD HAVE DONE IT DIFFERENTLY. I SHOULD HAVE SAT HER DOWN YEARS AGO AND JUST TALKED IT OUT. I SHOULD HAVE GOTTEN IT OUT OF MY SYSTEM INSTEAD OF BEING SO SECRETIVE ABOUT IT. I SHOULD HAVE TOLD HER THE DAY IT HAPPENED THAT I FELT BETRAYED AND ANGRY, AND THAT I FELT AS THOUGH I COULDN'T TRUST HER ANYMORE. WHY DIDN'T I JUST TELL HER? WELL, IT'S TOO LATE; I HAVE GONE TOO FAR. I CAN'T GO BACK AND CHANGE THINGS NOW. IT IS WHAT IT IS!

<<*Ring…ring…ring*>>. "Hello…hello," I said as I rolled over in the bed reaching for the phone.

"What you still doing in the bed?" Melvin said in a surprised tone.

"What? It's Sunday, it's cold, football season is over, and I have the house to myself. Unless you know something I don't, I don't see a reason to get outta bed! The question is, why are you calling my house so early? Don't you got a girl yet?", I asked jokingly as I readjusted the covers.

"I'm lifting weights and I need someone to spot me," Melvin replied.

"Why didn't you say that in the first place? Give me thirty. I need to hop in the shower real quick and throw some gear on." I jumped out of the bed, grabbed a pair of all red Lathrup High jogging pants, my red Lathrup hoodie, a pair of socks, a white t-shirt, my underwear, and headed for the bathroom.

Suddenly, I heard a noise coming from downstairs. It sounded like someone opening the garage door, but that was impossible. My parents were in Chicago visiting my aunt Wanda. Then I heard loud footsteps moving toward the living room. My heart was pounding so loud I was afraid the intruder could hear it.

My adrenaline started to kick in and I tiptoed back into my room, grabbed my baseball bat from under my bed, and headed toward the stairs. With the bat tightly clinched in both hands, I gently walked down each stair trying desperately not to make a sound. As I approached the last step, I turned my body toward the direction where I heard the sound and out of the corner of my eye I saw a large male frame standing in the living room area. I walked slowly toward the figure with the bat at my side, ready to swing and bring whoever it was to the ground. I bent down trying to stay low when suddenly, the image became clear. It was my father. But that could not be, he was supposed to be in Chicago with my mother. I stopped dead in my tracks, did an about face, and ran back up the stairs. With each step my heart pounded harder and harder. Once I made it to the top of the stairs I shot into my room, grabbed the phone and called Melvin back. "Dog, you're not going to believe this my father's at the crib!" "I thought you said they were in Chicago?" "I thought they were too, but apparently he's not. I think he's been here the entire weekend." "Alright, calm down, just calm down, whatever you do don't panic, just act normal. He probably doesn't even know," Melvin whispered. "You right, I put all the beer bottles in the garbage, put everything back like I found it and I cleaned the house pretty good. You're right, I'm trippin, he didn't notice. We did trash all the bottles and clean the grill, right?" Melvin was quiet.

Once I got off the phone with Melvin I quickly hopped in the shower. When I got out I threw on my jogging pants and hoodie, headed down the stairs and out the door. I was half way out of the door when suddenly I heard him call my name. "Eric, do you know what your mother did with the steak?" "What steak?" I replied without hesitation. I headed toward the kitchen trying to keep a straight face. I kept thinking about what Melvin said, "Stay calm and act like nothing happened." "Are you sure you have no idea what your mother did with the steak?" "Yes sir, she didn't mention anything to me about no steak." "All right," he said. "I'm about to go over Melvin's for a while." I walked out of the door slowly as to suggest everything was normal, but I knew if they found out I threw a party at the house and barbequed the steak, I was a dead man walking. I had a feeling my father didn't buy my story and as soon as my mom got home from

Chicago he was going to check with her to find out what really happened. If they put all the pieces together, I was going to have to get out of the house before my father killed me.

"Stop being so paranoid. You know how mean your old dude is, if he thought for one second we had a party at the house last night, he would have murdered you by now," Melvin said jokingly. "You haven't said a word since you been here. For real E, you need to chill out. Tomorrow morning everything will be back to normal." <<*Ring...ring...*>> "Hello, how are you?" Melvin's mom said as she picked up the phone.

 I got quiet and went to the stairwell so I could hear Mrs. Brown's conversation. I can't explain it, but somehow I just knew that it was my mother on the other end of the phone. My heart started racing again. It was early evening and that was around the time my mom generally made it in whenever she drove home from Chicago. Also, the tone in Melvin's mother's voice didn't sound like she was speaking to a close friend.

"As a matter of fact they were together late last night," she told the person on the other end. "Not a problem, have a good evening, I'll talk to you soon." "Eric, that was your mother, she wants you to come home."

"I knew it! I knew it. I shouldn't have listened to you. I knew I shouldn't have thrown a party at the crib," I said while pacing the floor. "We probably left all kind of evidence. Man, he is about to kill me. I knew I shouldn't have listened to ya'll fools."

"Stop acting like a punk and calm down. You want me to go with you?"

Trying to impress Melvin, I lied, "Naw, I ain't scared of that dude. Let me get my jacket. I'm good. I'll call you if I need you."

"You know I got your back," Melvin said sincerely. Even though I knew he had my back, I was not in the least bit comforted by his words. He didn't have to face my father, I did. On the way home I cut through the neighbor's yard taking my usual shortcut, but then backtracked and took the scenic route. It didn't make a lot of sense to rush home for a butt whipping. As I walked toward the house I told myself, "Party or no party, right or wrong, he wasn't going to put his hands on me again." I was the only kid on the block still getting whippings in high school. I was 16 and still had to wear long-sleeved shirts to school to hide the bruises on my arm that I got from trying to protect myself from the belt. It actually looked worse than it felt. What hurt the most was the fact that my classmates would joke on me about it. When I walk in this house if any one of them says something about me getting a whipping, it's on!

As I grabbed the knob on the screen door and walked through the garage into the house, I kept telling myself to relax and act normal. I deliberately went through the garage and not the front door because it gave me a few extra minutes to gather myself. I paused for about 30 seconds to calm down, gain my composure, and practice saying, "What's up ma, Mrs. Brown said you wanted to talk to me." I must have practiced saying, "What up ma, Mrs. Brown said you wanted to talk to me," a million times before I mustered up enough courage to walk into the house, and into the family room to face my parents.

As I walked into the family room, the sight of my parents struck fear in my heart. I opened my mouth and all the moisture evaporated and my voice began to crack, "Mrs. Bbbbbbrown, I stuttered, ssssaid you wanted to see me."

"Yes, I talked with your dad yesterday and he said that the steak was missing. Do you know what happened to it?

"No ma'am."

"Well, that's strange because your father and I found beer bottles in the backyard and the grill looks like someone cooked steak on it recently. I am going to try this again! Did you have a party here last night?", she pressed.

"Party? No ma'am, I didn't have a party here last night." I tried to keep a straight face, but it was difficult because my mom always knew when I was lying.

"Stop lying. Eric, I am so damn sick of you. How could you have a party in my house, eat the groceries your father and I worked for, and have absolute strangers in my house? What in the hell were you thinking?", she screamed. I didn't say a word; I just stared at her.

"Eric, do you hear me talking to you? I asked you a question, what in the hell were you thinking? I want an answer and I want it now!" I didn't flinch, I just stood there with a blank look on my face.

"Son, your mother asked you a question," he chimed in. I pretended as if I did not hear a word he was saying. "I know you hear me talking to you son...I said your mother asked you a question!" He typically used a different tone of voice when he had to repeat himself. He was from the old school and believed that when an adult spoke to a child, the child was supposed to acknowledge he or she was being spoken to. I knew the drill. If you did not respond the first time, he would ask you a second time a bit louder, giving you the benefit of the doubt that maybe you didn't hear him. He was not necessarily trying to scare you by projecting his voice; it was more of a warning. Generally, I would surrender. I would play the dumb role like I did not hear him the first time, and the second time say, "yes sir" and answer the question. Not this time. In a strong and demanding voice he said, "Boy, you better answer your mother." Before I knew it I snapped and my mind went blank. I was physically in the room, but mentally I was long gone.

"You can't make me," I murmured under my breath as I bit my bottom lip and shook my head as if to say "not this time—not this time."

Welcome to
Breathe University™

A holistic approach to success, involving a series of one on one intimate instructional sessions with Inspirational Speaker and Life Strategist, Eric Thomas, to help you transform your life in the areas of: Finances, Relationships, Career Goals, Marriage and more!

For more information contact:
info@BreatheUniversity.com or call 866-526-3978

Eric Thomas & Associates

EXPECT ASCENSION

Education Consulting
Athletic Development
Executive Coaching
Professional Development

When you want to succeed as bad as you want to breathe...®

www.ETinspires.com   Eric Thomas & Associates, LLC.   866.526.3978

GREATNESS IS UPON YOU
Success Journal

Follow along with ET on a more intimate and thought provoking level! Get bonus activities and exercises, summary notes and more with the GIUY Success Journal!

shop.ETinspires.com   Eric Thomas & Associates, LLC.   866.526.3978

Let's get social!

Facebook:
ETTheHipHopPreacher

Twitter:
@EricThomasBTC
@ET_Inspires

Instagram:
@ETTheHipHopPreacher
@ET_Inspires

www.ETinspires.com Eric Thomas & Associates, LLC 866.526.3978

SPIRIT REIGN
PUBLISHING
A Division of Spirit Reign Communications